# IPHONE 15 PRO AND PRO MAX USER GUIDE

## Your step-by-step ultimate companion for beginners and seniors

## By

## Ethan Quill

# Table of Contents

iv

# INTRODUCTION

## iPhone 15 Pro Model's Specification

### Network Technology:

GSM / CDMA / HSPA / EVDO / LTE / 5G

### Launch:

- Announced: September 12, 2023

- Status: Available, released on the 22nd /09/2023

**Body:**

- Dimensions: 146. 6 x 70. 6 x 8. 3 mm (5. 77 x 2. 78 x 0. 33 in)

- Weight: 187 g (6. 60 oz)

- Construction: Glass front (Corning Glass), glass back (Corning Glass), titanium frame (grade 5)

**SIM:**

- Nano-SIM and eSIM (International)

- Multi-digit dual eSIM (US)

- Dual SIM (Nano-SIM, dual standby) (China)

- IP rating: Dustproof and IP68 water (up to 6 m for 30 minutes)

- Apple Pay: Visa, MasterCard, AMEX Certified

## Display:

- Type: LTPO Super Retina XDR OLED, 120 Hz

- Size: 6, 1 inch

- Resolution: 1179 x 2556 pixels, 19. 5:9 ratio (density ~ 461 ppi)

- Protection: Ceramic Shield glass

- Features: always-on display

## Platform:

- OS: iOS 17, can upgrade to iOS 17. 4,

- Chipset: Apple A17 Pro (3 nm)

- CPU: Hexa-core (2x3. 78 GHz + 4x2. 11 GHz)

- GPU: Apple GPU (6-core graphics)

## Memory:

- Memory card slot: No.

- Internal memory: 128 GB RAM 8 GB, 256 GB RAM 8 GB, 512 GB RAM 8 GB, 1 TB RAM 8 GB

- Storage type: NVMe

## Main camera:

- Triple configuration:

- 48 MP wide

- 12 MP telephoto lens

- 12 MP ultra-wide

- TOF (depth) 3D LiDAR scanner

- Features: Dual two-color LED flash, HDR (photo/panorama)

- Video: 4K at 24/25/30/60 fps, 1080p at 25/30/60/120/240 fps, 10-bit HDR, Dolby Vision HDR

**Selfie camera:**

- Single configuration: 12 Wide MP

- SL 3D (depth sensor/biometric)

- Features: HDR, cinematic mode (4K at 24/30 fps)

- Video: 4K at 24/25/30/60 fps, 1080p at 25/30/60/120 fps

**Audio:**

- Speaker: Yes, with stereo speakers

- 3. 5 mm jack: No

**Connectivity:**

- WLAN: Wi-Fi 802. 11 a/b/g/n/ac/ 6e, band Dual frequency, hotspot - Bluetooth: 5. 3, A2DP, LE

- Positioning: GPS (L1+L5), GLONASS, GALILEO, BDS, QZSS, NavIC

- NFC: Yes

- Radio: No

- USB: USB Type-C 3. 2 Gen 2, DisplayPort

## Features:

- Sensors: Face ID, accelerometer, gyroscope, proximity, compass, barometer

- Supports Ultra-Wideband 2 (UWB)

- Emergency SOS via satellite

(send/receive SMS)

**Battery:**

- Type: Li-Ion 3274 mAh, non-removable

- Charging: Wired, PD2. 0, 15W Wireless

(MagSafe), 15W No wired (Qi2 - requires

iOS 17. 2 update), 4. 5 W wired reverse

**Others:**

- Color: Black Titanium, White Titanium,

Blue Titanium, Natural Titanium

- Model: A2848 , A3101, A3102, A3104, iPhone16. 1

- SAR (Specific Absorption Rate):

- Head: 1. 14 W/kg

- Legion: 1. 16 W/kg

- DAS UE:

- Tête: 0. 98 W/kg

- Legion: 0. 98 W/kg

- Price: $ 849. 95 / € 1 055. 99 / £833. 90 / ☐127,990

**Test:**

- Display: Contrast Ratio: Infinite
(nominal)

- Camera: Photo / Video

- Speaker: -26. 4 LUFS (Good)

- Battery life: Active use score 12:58h,
endurance rating 86h

# iPhone 15 Pro Max Model's Specification

## Network Technology:

GSM / CDMA / HSPA / EVDO / LTE / 5G

## Notice:

Announced September 12, 2023

## Available:

Released September 22, 2023

## Body:

- Dimensions: 159. 9 x 76. 7 x 8. 3 mm (6

,30 x 3. 02 x 0. 33 in)

- Weight**: 221 g (7. 80 oz)

- Construction: Glass front (Corning

Glass), glass back (Corning Glass) ,

titanium frame (grade 5)


**SIM:**

- Nano-SIM and eSIM (International)

- Multi-number dual eSIM (US)

- Dual SIM (Nano-SIM, dual standby)

(China)


**IP rating:**

- IP68 dust and water resistant (up to 6 m for 30 minutes)

## Apple Pay:

- Visa, MasterCard, AMEX certified

## Display:

- Type: LTPO Super Retina 17, upgradeable to iOS 17. 4

- Chipset: Apple A17 Pro (3 nm)

- Processor: Hexa-core (2x3. 78 GHz + 4x2. 11 GHz)

- GPU: Apple GPU (6-core graphics)

**Memory:**

- Card slots: No

- Internal memory: 256 GB RAM 8 GB,

512 RAM GB 8 GB RAM, 1 TB 8 GB RAM

- Storage type: NVMe

**Main camera:**

- Triple configuration:

- 48 MP wide

- 12 MP periscope telephoto lens

- Angle ultra-wide 12 MP

- TOF 3D LiDAR scanner (depth)

## Selfie camera:

- Simple configuration: 12 MP wide

- SL 3D (depth/biometric sensor)

## Audio:

- High speaker: Yes, with stereo speaker

- 3. 5mm jack: No

## Connectivity:

- WLAN: Wi-Fi 802. 11 a/b/ g/n/ac/6e, dual band, hotspot

- Bluetooth: 5. 3, A2DP, LE

- GPS: Yes

- NFC: Yes

- USB: USB Type-C 3. 2 Gen 2,
DisplayPort


**Features:**

- Sensors: Face ID, accelerometer,
gyroscope, proximity, compass,
barometer

- Ultra Wideband 2 (UWB) supported

- Emergency SOS via satellite
(send/receive SMS)


**Battery:**

- Type: Li-Ion 4441 mAh, non-removable

- Charging: Wired (PD2. 0, 50% in 30 min), 15 W wireless (MagSafe), 15 W wireless (Qi2 - requires iOS 17. 2 update), 4. 5 W reversible wired

## Colors:

- Black Titanium, White Titanium, Blue Titanium, Natural Titanium

## Model:

- A2849, A3105, A3106, A3108, iPhone16. 2

**SAR (Specific Absorption Rate):**

- Head: 1. 07 W/kg

- Body: 1. 11 W/kg

**DAS UE:**

- Tête: 0. 98 W/kg

- Legion: 0. 98 W/kg

**Price:**

- $ 1,055. 59 / € 1,185 0 . 20 / £ 950. 00 / ☐148,900,

**Benchmark:**

- AnTuTu: 1487203 (v10)

- Geek Bench: 7237 (v6. 0)

## Speaker:

- 24. 5 LUFS (Very good)

## Battery life:

- Active usage score: 16:01h

- Endurance index: 118h

# Setting Up Your iPhone Basics

It's easy to get started with your iPhone thanks to the simple setup process. Whether you're diving into the experience for the first time or making sure you have all the essentials prepared, you're on the right track.

The Settings screen offers several options for transferring your apps and data. You can seamlessly transfer from an iCloud backup, another iPhone, a Mac or PC, an Android device, or choose not to transfer anything at all.

## Transferring your apps and information to your new iPhone

When you turn on your new iPhone and begin setting it up, you can effortlessly transfer many of your apps, settings, and content wirelessly from your old iPhone. Simply put the two devices together and follow the on-screen instructions.

## Connect to cellular services and Wi-Fi

Depending on the model, you can use an eSIM from your carrier or install a physical SIM card to connect to your cellular network. Check your iPhone's connection to your cellular plan by going to Settings > Cellular.

To connect your iPhone to your home Wi-Fi network, go to Settings > Wi-Fi, turn on Wi-Fi, and select your network. Your iPhone automatically connects to your Wi-Fi network when you're at home. Sign in with your Apple ID .

Your Apple ID is essential for accessing several Apple services, including Apple Music, FaceTime, iCloud and iMessage. If you don't have an Apple ID yet, you can easily create one.

To sign in with your Apple ID, go to Settings > Sign in on your iPhone. To confirm your login status, go to Settings > [Your Name]; Your Apple ID should appear under your name.

## Set up Face ID or Touch ID

Improve the security of your iPhone by setting up Face ID (face recognition) or Touch ID (fingerprint recognition). These features enable secure unlocking, app login and purchases. For added security, Face ID and Touch ID data remains solely on your device and is not stored anywhere else.

Depending on your iPhone model, follow these steps:

- Set up Face ID: Go to Settings > Face ID & Password, tap Set up Face ID, and follow the on-screen instructions.

- Touch ID settings: Go to Settings > Touch ID & password, tap Add fingerprint, and follow the on-screen instructions.

**Enable Find My iPhone.**

Make sure you can locate your iPhone if it is lost or stolen by turning on Find My

iPhone. Go to Settings > [your name] >
Find My iPhone, tap Find My iPhone, and
turn on Find My iPhone. You can track
the location of your devices via the Find
My app. If you can't access the app, you
can still find your device using Find My
on iCloud. com.

## iCloud Data Storage

Keep your important information safe
and synced across all your devices with
iCloud. If you replace, lose, or damage
your iPhone, your photos, videos, and
more will remain securely stored in
iCloud.

To enable or change the iCloud features you want to use, go to Settings > [your name] > iCloud.

# SEE WHAT'S NEW IN IOS

# 17

**StandBy:**

Improve your charging experience by rotating iPhone horizontally to remotely access essential information. Turn your device into a convenient bedside clock, browse photos easily, manage music playback, and more. Learn how StandBy easily improves your charging habits.

**Interactive Widgets:**

Enhance the functionality of widgets on the home screen, lock screen, and standby with new interactive capabilities. Simply tap a widget to complete tasks like completing quests, controlling home accessories, or enjoying the latest podcast episode. Unleash the potential of interactive widgets to streamline your daily operations.

**Contact posters:**

Personalize your calling experience by creating unique contact posters that recipients can see when calls come in. Make a lasting impression by creating a personalized display that reflects your identity. Learn how to add or edit your special contact posters to enrich your communications.

**Live voicemail:**

Stay informed with live transcriptions of voicemails as they are recorded. Get immediate context for incoming calls, allowing for quick action if necessary. Experience the convenience of live voicemail recording, available in the US and Canada.

**Stickers:**

Express your creativity with stickers, add style to photos, screenshots and more. Easily integrate stickers into your digital chats, whether they're Memoji creations or custom images. Immerse yourself in the world of stickers to improve your texting experience.

## Journal (iOS 17. 2):

Start your journey of self-discovery with the new Journal app, designed to easily cultivate a journaling habit. Organize outings, photo shoots, exercise, etc. With curated journaling suggestions, cultivate meaningful reflections on your daily experiences.

**Messages:**

Notify your connections when checking in, letting friends and family know when you've arrived safely. Seamlessly share your location in a Messages conversation or ask friends where they are. Explore advanced message filtering and transcription features for better communication efficiency.

**Keyboard:**

Control your text entry with temporary underlining of automatically corrected words, ensuring your messages are clear and precise. Apply inline predictive text suggestions as you type, streamlining your typing experience to increase productivity.

**FaceTime:**

Leave audio or video messages for missed FaceTime calls, enriching your communication options. Enhance your FaceTime conversations with expressive hand gestures, adding snappy responses to your calls. Seamlessly switch FaceTime calls between your iPhone and Apple TV for an uninterrupted connection.

## AirDrop:

Simplify contact sharing with NameDrop, making it easier to exchange contact information when you bring your iPhone together. Start AirDrop transfers or SharePlay sessions with ease, improving collaboration and sharing experiences.

## AirPlay (iOS 17. 3):

Immerse yourself in a personalized entertainment experience with AirPlay at select hotels, seamlessly streaming content from your iPhone to compatible TVs. Enhance your hotel stay with your favorite shows, music and memories right at your fingertips.

**Maps:**

Easily navigate offline by saving map areas directly to your iPhone for offline exploration. Optimize your trip in an electric vehicle with real-time charging station availability and charging network priority selection. Harness the full potential of Maps for a seamless navigation experience.

**Visual Search:**

Dig deeper into your visual content with Visual Lookup, identifying foods in photos or videos and suggesting related recipes. Better understand the objects in photos, enriching your visual storytelling skills.

**Photos:**

Celebrate your four-legged friends with pet identification, organizing them with your friends and family in the People & Pets album. Customize vertical focus points, rearrange mementos, and add flexibility to your photo organization efforts.

## Health:

Prioritize your emotional health through tracking your thoughts, allowing you to develop your emotional awareness and resilience. Access mental health resources and assessments directly in the Health app, making it easier for you to make more informed decisions about your health.

## Fitness:

Stay motivated and connected with friends with a redesigned Share tab that highlights achievements and milestones. Tailor your fitness journey with personalized workout and meditation plans in Apple Fitness+, optimizing your wellness routine for maximum effectiveness.

## Screen Distance:

Protect your visual health with Screen Distance during Screen Time, which encourages optimal viewing distance for extended device use. Promote healthy screen habits with personalized

distancing recommendations.

**Safari:**

Efficiently manage your browsing

activities with separate profiles for

distinct topics, ensuring privacy and

organization. Streamline the password

verification process with the ability to

autofill codes received in the mail. Makes

it easy to share passwords with people

you trust for added security and

convenience.

**Privacy and security:**

Apply advanced protections with Communication Safety, which provides protection against sensitive media content across a variety of platforms. Improve your device's resilience to cyber threats with Lockdown Mode, strengthening your digital security defenses.

**Accessibility:**

Empower people with voice loss with Personal Voice, facilitating natural communication with Direct Speech. Simplify text interactions for the visually impaired with Point and Talk, allowing

seamless interaction with labeled objects.

**Reminder:**

Streamline your shopping experience

with Grocery List, which intelligently

categorizes items for improved

organization. Improve task management

with divided lists and column views,

bringing clarity and efficiency to your

reminders.

**Notes:**

Seamlessly integrate PDFs and scans into your notes, centralizing your references for easy access. Promote connectivity between related notes with hyperlinks, promoting seamless navigation and organization in your digital workspace.

**Freeform:**

Get creative with new drawing tools, including watercolor brushes, calligraphy pens, and more. Take advantage of the flexibility of Freeform boards for collaborative brainstorming and creative expression.

## Find My:

Enhance collaboration and tracking with shared AirTags and Find My, allowing multiple users to locate and monitor their belongings. Simplify meetings with precise instructions in the Find My ecosystem, facilitating seamless coordination.

## News:

Engage your mind with daily crossword puzzles in the Apple News app, enriching your reading experience with interactive challenges. Immerse yourself in Apple

News+ audio stories, now accessible directly in the Podcasts app

## Home:

Activity History lets you see who locked or unlocked the door and when. It also shows recent activity from your garage door, contact sensors, and security system.

*Note:* New features and apps may vary depending on your model, region, language, and service provider.

# SETUP AND GET

# STARTED WITH IPHONE

Getting started with your new iPhone is simple and straightforward. Whether you're setting up for the first time or transferring data from another device, follow these simple steps to get started.

### Preparing Setup

Before you begin setting up iPhone, make sure you have the following ready:

- Connect to the Internet via Wi-Fi or cellular data service

- Your Apple ID and password (or create one during setup)

- Credit or debit card information if you want to add a card to Apple Pay

- Old iPhone or backup if you're transferring data

data - Your Android device if you are transferring content from it

# Turn On and Set Up Your iPhone

## 1. Turn on your iPhone

Turn on your iPhone by pressing and holding the side button until the Apple logo appears appear [Green arrow points to the button next to it]

If your iPhone won't turn on, you may need to charge it.

*Pro Tip:* If you are visually impaired, use VoiceOver or Zoom accessibility by triple-clicking the side or home button.

## 2. Choose setup method:

- *Quick Start:* If you have another iOS device, use Quick Start to automatically transfer settings and preferences. Follow the instructions on the screen.

*- Configure Manually:* If you don't have another device, tap "Configure Manually" and follow the on-screen instructions.

## Moving from an Android device

If you're moving from an Android device, you can transfer your data using the Move to iOS app during setup:

1. On your device your Android, make sure Wi-Fi is turned on and open the Move to iOS app.

2. Follow the on-screen instructions to start the transfer process.

3. On your iPhone, select "From Android" when prompted during setup.

4. Follow the setup wizard and select the data you want to transfer from your Android device.

*Note:* If you completed setup without using Move to iOS, you may need to erase iPhone or transfer data manually.

With these steps, you'll have your new iPhone up and running in no time!

# Wake And Unlock Your iPhone

Your iPhone saves power by turning off the screen and locking it for security. When you're ready to use it again, you can quickly wake and unlock your iPhone using different methods.

## Wake your iPhone:

To wake iPhone, you can do one of the following:

1. Press the side button on the right edge of iPhone.

2. Pick up your iPhone and it will automatically wake up from sleep. (To turn this feature off, go to Settings > Display & Brightness and turn off "Raise to wake.")

3. Tap the screen to wake (not available on iPhone SE).

**Unlock with Face ID:**

If your iPhone supports Face ID and you've set it up, unlocking is easy:

1. Wake your iPhone by tapping the screen or lifting it.

2. Look at your iPhone to activate Face ID.

3. Once iPhone recognizes your face, the
   lock icon will change from closed to
   open, indicating that the device is
   unlocked. 4. Swipe up from the
   bottom of the screen to return to the
   Home screen.

To re-lock your iPhone, press the side
button. It will also automatically lock
after one minute of inactivity unless
"Attention Feature" is enabled in Settings
> Face ID & Passcode.

**Unlocking with Touch ID:**

For iPhones with Home button and
Touch ID, unlocking is done as follows:

1. Press the Home button with your
   Touch ID-registered finger.
2. Your iPhone will unlock if it
   recognizes your fingerprint.
3. To lock again, press the side button. It
   will also automatically lock after one
   minute of inactivity.

**Unlock with a passcode:**

If you haven't set up Touch ID or Face
ID, you can unlock iPhone with a
passcode:

1. Swipe up from the bottom of the lock screen (Face ID) or press the Home button (other models) to access the passcode screen.

2. Enter the password using the keyboard.

3. Your iPhone will unlock if the correct passcode is entered.

4. To lock again, press the side button. It will also automatically lock after one minute of inactivity.

# Set up cellular service on iPhone

To connect to a cellular network, your iPhone needs a physical SIM card or eSIM. Here's how to set up mobile service:

1. **Contact your service provider:** Contact your service provider to get a SIM card and activate mobile service dynamic. Note that available options may vary depending on your iPhone model and location. For iPhones purchased in the United States. Starting from iPhone 14, only eSIM is supported.

## 2. Set up eSIM:

- If your carrier supports eSIM activation, follow the onscreen instructions when setting up iPhone.

- Alternatively, if setup is complete, you can:

- Activate eSIM via carrier: Follow the instructions provided by your carrier or go to Settings > Cellular > Setup mobile or Add eSIM.

- Use eSIM Quick Transfer: transfer your phone number from old iPhone to new iPhone wirelessly. Both devices must be

running iOS 16 or later.

## 3. Use QR code:

If your carrier offers QR codes, go to

Settings > Cellular > Set up cellular

network or Add eSIM > Use QR code

and follow the prompts.

## 4. Switching from another

## smartphone:

Contact your carrier if your old device

is not an iPhone.

**5. Activate via carrier's application:**
Download the carrier's application
from the App Store and follow the
instructions to activate mobile service.

To set up eSIM, make sure your iPhone is
connected to the Internet via Wi-Fi or a
cellular network.

**6. Insert physical SIM card:**

- Get a nano-SIM card from your
  carrier or transfer a card from your
  old iPhone.

- Use a paper clip or SIM ejector to
  open the SIM tray. Insert the SIM

card into the tray, then reinsert it into your iPhone.

- If prompted, enter the SIM card PIN.

## 7. Convert physical SIM to eSIM:

- If supported by your carrier, go to Settings > Cellular > Set up cellular network or Add eSIM, select physical SIM and tap "Switch to eSIM".

*Note:* Don't forget to factor in data, voice and roaming charges, especially when traveling. Additionally, some carriers offer the ability to unlock your iPhone for

use with other carriers for an additional

fee.

# Using Dual SIM on iPhone

The Dual SIM feature on iPhone offers many different conveniences, allowing you to effectively manage multiple numbers and data packages. Here's how to get the most out of dual SIM:

1. **Business and personal calls:** Assign one number for work purposes and another number for personal purposes.

2. **Travel Data Plan:** Add a local data plan when traveling to different countries or regions.

## 3. Dedicated voice and data plan:

Choose your own voice and data plan according to your needs.

## To configure dual SIM:

## 1. Compatibility:

Check if your iPhone supports dual SIM. You can use:

- One physical SIM and one eSIM on selected models.
- Two eSIMs on specific iPhone versions.

## 2. Settings:

- Go to Settings > Mobile networks and make sure you have at least two lines.

- Add lines if needed by following the cell service setup process.

## 3. Activate:

- Activate both lines by tapping each line and selecting "Activate this line".

- Customize settings like cellular plan label, Wi-Fi calling, calling on another device, or SIM PIN.

## 4. Data and voice options:

- Choose the default line for mobile data and voice calls.

- Turn on "Allow mobile data switching" to use either line depending on coverage and availability.

### Note when using dual SIM:

- *Wi-Fi calling:* Turn on the Wi-Fi calling feature to receive calls without interruption on both lines.

- *Missed call:* Calls on a line without Wi-Fi calling will be sent to voicemail if the other line is in use.

- *Call forwarding:* Configure conditional call forwarding for busy or idle lines, if supported by your service provider.

- *Multi-device call:* Phone calls made from other devices use the default voice line on your iPhone.
- *Messaging:* Remember that SMS/MMS conversations are tied to the selected line and cannot be switched mid-conversation.
- *Use hotspot:* Instant and personal hotspots use the selected line for mobile data.

**Note:** Remember to check your carrier's terms and conditions, especially about roaming fees and additional charges. Dual

SIM offers flexibility that allows you to

effectively manage your iPhone

communication needs.

# Connect iPhone to the Internet

To access the Internet on iPhone, you can connect to your service provider's Wi-Fi network or cellular network. Here's how:

## Connect to a Wi-Fi network:

1. Open Settings and tap Wi-Fi

2. Toggle the Wi-Fi switch to turn it on.

3. Select a network from the available list:

   - Select the network and enter the password if prompted.

- For hidden networks, tap "More" and enter network details manually.

4. Once connected, the Wi-Fi icon will appear at the top of the screen.

## Join Personal Hotspot:

1. Go to Settings > Wi-Fi

2. Select the device name sharing Personal Hotspot.

3. Enter the password shown in Settings > Mobile > Personal Hotspot on the shared device.

4. Your iPhone will connect to the shared mobile Internet connection.

## Connect to a mobile network:

1. Make sure your SIM card is activated and unlocked.

2. Go to Settings > Cellular and verify that cellular data is turned on.

3. For Dual SIM users, select the priority line for mobile data.

4. First, iPhone tries to connect to Wi-Fi. If not available, iPhone connects to the cellular network.

*Note:* On compatible iPhones that support 5G, the device may prioritize 5G mobile data over Wi-Fi. You can switch back to Wi-Fi by going to Network

Settings.

# Sign in with your Apple ID on iPhone

Your Apple ID serves as a gateway to various Apple services like the App Store, iTunes Store, iCloud, and more.

**To sign in with your Apple ID:**

1. Go to Settings.
2. Tap "Connect to your iPhone."

Then follow one of these steps:

- Sign in with a nearby iPhone or iPad: Select "Use another Apple device" and follow the onscreen instructions.

- Sign in manually using your address email or phone number only.
- Select "Sign in manually" and enter your Apple ID information. If you don't have an Apple ID, you can create one.

If two-factor authentication is turned on, enter the code six-digit verification.

## Adjust Apple ID settings

1. Go to Settings > [your name].
2. Here you can:
   - Update your contact details

- Change your password

- Add or remove account recovery
  contacts

- Use iCloud services

- Manage your subscriptions

- Update your payment method or
  billing address

- Control Family Sharing settings

# Using iCloud on iPhone

iCloud serves as a secure storage solution for photos, videos, documents, backups and more, ensuring they stay updated automatically across all Apple devices. Additionally, iCloud lets you share a variety of items such as photos, calendars, notes, folders, and files with your contacts. It offers an email account and offers 5GB of free storage, with the option to subscribe to iCloud+ for additional features and storage.

*Note:* Some iCloud features may have specific system requirements and availability that may vary by country or region.

**1. Adjust iCloud settings**

1. Sign in with your Apple ID, then do the following:

2. Go to Settings > [your name] > iCloud.

3. Here you can:

   - Check your iCloud storage status.

   - Enable features like Photos, iCloud Drive, and iCloud Backup.

**How to use iCloud on iPhone**

1. iCloud can automatically back up your iPhone.

2. Store a variety of information in iCloud and sync across your Apple devices, including:

   - Photos and videos: Use iCloud Photos.

   - Files and Documents: Set up iCloud Drive.

   - iCloud Mail

   - Contacts, calendars, notes, and reminders

   - Data from compatible third-party apps and games

   - Messages: configure messages on iPhone.

- Passwords and payment methods: Use iCloud Keychain.

- Safari Bookmarks and Open Tabs: Organize tabs in Safari.

- News, stocks and weather settings

- Family and health data

- Voice memos

- Favorite maps

## Additional functions:

- Photo and video sharing: create albums share or join an iCloud shared photo library.

- Share folders and documents using iCloud Drive: Learn how to share files and folders in iCloud Drive.

- Use Find My to locate your device or share your location with friends and family.

- Sign up for iCloud+ for more storage and features like iCloud Private Forwarding, Hide My Email, and HomeKit Secure Video support.

*Note:* You can access your iCloud data on a variety of devices, including iPad,

Apple Watch, Mac, Apple TV, Windows computers, and iCloud.com.

# Charging and Monitoring the Battery

## Charging your iPhone

Your iPhone is equipped with an internal rechargeable lithium-ion battery, providing optimal performance for your device. Compared to traditional battery technology, lithium-ion batteries are lighter, charge faster, last longer and have increased lifespan.

## About charging the battery

- There is a lightning bolt on the battery icon, which means the battery is being charged.
- The battery icon in the upper right corner shows the battery level or charging status. When syncing or actively using iPhone, charging times may take longer.
- If your iPhone's battery is extremely low, the device may display a low battery image, indicating that the battery needs to be recharged for up to 10 minutes before you can use it. If the battery is extremely low, the screen may remain blank for up to 2 minutes

before the low battery image
appears.

## Charging methods

To charge your iPhone, consider the
following options:

- Connect your iPhone to a power
  outlet using the included charging
  cable and Apple USB power
  adapter or compatible mains power
  source with adapter (sold
  separately).
- Place your iPhone face up on the
  MagSafe Charger, MagSafe Charger
  Duo (connected to the Apple 20W

USB-C Power Adapter or other compatible power adapter), or Qi-certified charger (all sold private). Access MagSafe chargers and batteries for iPhone and Qi-certified wireless chargers for iPhone.

- Use third-party power adapters and Qi-certified chargers that comply with applicable safety standards and regulations.

*Alternatively, you can connect your iPhone to your computer using a cable. Make sure your computer is turned on because charging will not take place if*

*the computer is turned off.*

**WARNING:** Avoid charging iPhone if you suspect there is liquid in the charging port.

## Optimize iPhone Battery Charging

iPhone offers a feature to slow battery aging by delaying charging beyond 80% until needed. This feature learns your charging habits through machine learning. To turn on Optimized Charging:

- On iPhone 14 and earlier, go to Settings > Battery > Health & Charging and turn on Optimized Charging.

- On iPhone 15 models, go to Settings > Battery > Battery Health & Charging, tap Optimized Charging, and select Optimized Charging.

## Battery care and low power mode

Monitor battery health and performance by going to Settings > Battery > Battery health and charge. Adjust settings like Clean Energy Charging (available in the

US.), predicts carbon emissions to optimize charging.

Also, use power saving mode to extend battery life in low power situations. This mode reduces power consumption for important tasks, although performance may be affected.

**To enable power saving mode:**

- In Settings: Go to Settings > Battery.
- In Control Center: Open Control Center and tap the Power Saver button.

*Tips:* To add the Power Saver button to Control Center, go to Settings > Control Center and customize it accordingly.

# IPHONE BASICS

Learn basic gestures to interact with your iPhone:

**Tap:**

Quickly tap an item on the screen with one finger. For example, tap an app icon on the Home screen to open that app.

**Press and hold:**

Tap an item on the screen until there is a response. For example, tap and hold the wallpaper on the home screen to launch the app icon wiggle mode.

## Drag:

Move one finger quickly on the screen. For example, swipe left on the Home screen to access more apps.

## Scroll:

Slide one finger across the screen without lifting it. For example, in Photos, drag the list up or down to see more items. Swipe to scroll quickly and tap the screen to stop scrolling.

## Zoom:

Place two fingers close together on the screen. Spread them apart to zoom in, or move them together to zoom out.

*Alternatively, you can double-tap a photo or web page to zoom in and double-tap again to zoom out. In Maps, double-tap and hold, then drag up to zoom in or down to zoom out.*

# Adjusting the volume on iPhone

## Use physical buttons:

When you're on a call or listening to media, use the buttons on the side of the device to adjust the volume. Otherwise, these buttons control ringtones, alerts, and other sound effects. You can also use Siri to increase or decrease the volume by saying commands like "Volume up" or "Volume down."

## Lock ringer and alert volume:

In Settings, go to Sound & Haptics and turn off "Change with button" to prevent the volume buttons from changing ringer and alert volume.

**Control Center:**

Access Control Center when your iPhone is locked or when you are using the app to adjust the volume by dragging the volume slider.

**Reduce loud sounds from headphones:**

Go to Settings > Sound & Feeling >
Headphone Safety, turn on "Reduce Loud
Sounds" and adjust the slider to specify
the maximum volume for protection your
hearing.

**Temporarily mute calls, alerts, and
notifications:**

Open Control Center, tap Focus, then
select Do Not Disturb to temporarily
mute incoming calls, alerts, and
notifications.

**Silent mode:**

Go into silent mode by setting the Ring/Silent switch (or action button on iPhone 15 Pro and iPhone 15 Pro Max) to silent. In Settings > Sound & Haptics (on iPhone 15 Pro and iPhone 15 Pro Max), you can also turn on Silent mode.

*Note:* When Silent mode is turned on, iPhone will mute incoming calls, alerts, and sound effects, although the device may still vibrate. Note that some sounds, like alarm clocks and sounds from specific apps, can still be played through the built-in speaker, even in silent mode.

*Tips:* Be careful with headphone volume to protect your hearing: use the audiogram data in Health on iPhone to guide you.

# Opening Apps On iPhone

## From the Home screen:

- To access the Home screen, swipe up from the bottom edge of the screen (on iPhones with Face ID) or press the Home button (on iPhone). using the Home button).

- Swipe left or right to navigate different pages on the home screen.

- To quickly find apps, swipe left until you reach the App Library, where your apps are categorized.

- Tap the app icon you want to open.

## From App Library:

- Swipe from the bottom edge of the
  screen (on iPhone with Face ID) or
  press the Home button (on iPhone
  with Home button) to return to
  App Library.
- Tap on the desired app icon to open
  it.

**To find and open apps using the
App Library on iPhone, follow these
steps:**

**1. Go to App Library:**

- Go to Home screen and swipe left
  all the way to enter application.
  Library.

## 2. Search or browse for an app:

- Tap the search box at the top to search for a specific app by name.
- You can also scroll up and down to browse the alphabetical list of apps.

## 3. Open an app:

- Once you find the app you're looking for, tap its icon to open it.

If a category in the App Library contains multiple apps, you can tap the category to expand it and see all the apps in that category.

## To hide or show Home screen pages:

1. Touch and hold the Home screen until apps start to jiggle.

2. Tap the dots at the bottom to see thumbnail images of the pages on your Home screen.

3. To hide a page, clear the check mark below the page. To show a hidden page, add a check mark.

4. Tap "Done" (or press the Home button) to save your changes.

## To rearrange Home screen pages:

1. Touch and hold the Home screen until apps start to jiggle.

2. Tap the dots at the bottom to see thumbnail images of the pages on your Home screen.

3. Touch and hold a page, then drag it to a new location.

4. Tap "Done" twice (or press the Home button twice) to exit editing mode.

**To change where to download new apps:**

1. Go to Settings > Home & app library.

2. Choose whether the new app should be added to both the Home screen and App Library, or just the App Library.

## To move an app from the App Library to the Home screen:

1. Touch and hold the app in the App Library.
2. Tap "Add to home screen" if the app is not there yet.
3. The app will be added to both the home screen and the app library.

## Switch between open applications

To switch between open applications on your iPhone, you can use the App Switcher feature. Here's how:

## 1. Open the App Switcher:

- On an iPhone with Face ID: Swipe up from the bottom of the screen and pause in the middle.
- On an iPhone with a Home button: Double click the Home button.

## 2. Browse open apps:

- In App Switcher, you will see all your open apps displayed.
- Swipe right or left to browse open apps.

### 3. **Select the application to switch to:**

- Click on the application you want
  to switch to.

### 4. Quick switching between apps (Face ID only):

- On iPhones with Face ID, you can
  also swipe right or left along the
  bottom edge of the screen to
  quickly switch between open apps.

# Multitask With Picture in Picture

To multitask with Picture in Picture on iPhone, allowing you to watch videos or use FaceTime while using other apps, follow these steps:

## 1. Turn on Picture in Picture:

- While watching a video or while watching FaceTime. call, press the Video Cut button.

## 2. Interaction with the Picture-in-Picture window:

- The video window will shrink to a corner of the screen, allowing you to see the main screen and open other applications.

- You can resize the video window by opening or closing the video window.

-  Tap the video window to show or hide controls.

- Move the video window by dragging it to another corner of the screen.

- Hide the video window by dragging it off the left or right edge of the screen.

- Close the video window by pressing the Close button.

## 3. Restore full screen:

- To return to full screen view of the video, press the Restore full screen button in the small video window.

# Access Features and Information from Lock Screen

To access features and information from the iPhone lock screen, follow these steps:

## 1. Open Camera:

- Swipe left on the lock screen to quickly access the Camera app. On supported models, you can also press and hold the Camera button, then lift your finger.

## 2. Open Control Center:

- Swipe down from the upper right

  corner (on iPhones with Face ID)

  or swipe up from the bottom edge

  of the screen (on other iPhone

  models) to open Control Center.

  Here, you can access various

  settings and shortcuts.


**3. View earlier notifications:**

- Swipe up from the center of the

  Lock Screen to see notifications

  that you might have missed.


**4. View more widgets:**

- Swipe right on the Lock Screen to access additional widgets. These widgets provide quick access to information and actions in your favorite apps.

## 5. Media playback controls:

- Use playback controls (Now playing) on the lock screen to manage media playback, such as play, pause, rewind or fast-forward audio or video content quickly.

To customize what you can access from the lock screen, adjust your settings in

Control & Notification Center preferences. Additionally, you can choose how notification previews are displayed on the lock screen by configuring your notification settings. You can also view and control activities directly from the lock screen, including live sports updates, order updates and media playback. Additionally, you can control media playback on remote devices, such as Apple TV or HomePod, from your iPhone's lock screen.

# Perform Quick Actions on iPhone

Performing quick actions on iPhone allows you to navigate different tasks and apps efficiently. Here's how to perform quick actions from various locations:

## From the Home screen and App Library:

Press and hold an app icon to open quick actions in the menu application. For example:

- Touch and hold the Camera app to access options like "Take a selfie".

- Touch and hold Maps to select "Send my location".

- Touch and hold a Note to create a "New Note. "

**See previews and other quick action menus:**

- In Photos, tap and hold an image to preview and access a list of options.

- In Mail, tap and hold an image picture messages in your inbox to preview

- Open Control Center and touch and hold an item, such as the Camera button or brightness control, to see options

- On the lock screen, tap and hold a notification to respond directly to it
- While typing, press and hold the spacebar with one finger to turn the on-screen keyboard into a touchpad for navigation.

*Note:* If you hold an app icon for too long without selecting a quick action, all the app icons may start to shake. Just tap "Done" (on iPhones with Face ID) or press the Home button (on other iPhone models) to exit this mode and try again.

# Searching On Your iPhone

Searching with Spotlight on your iPhone allows quick access to a variety of content, apps, contacts, and more. Here's how to use Spotlight Search effectively:

## Select apps to include in your search:

- Go to Settings > Siri & Search.

- Scroll down and select an app.

- Enable "Show apps in search" option to include or exclude it from search results.

## Perform a search with iPhone:

- Tap the Search button at the bottom of the Home screen (on models with Face ID) or swipe down on the home screen or lock screen.
- Enter your search query in the search box.
- Search action:
- Start a search by pressing "Search" or "Go".
- Open a suggested app by tapping it.
- Perform quick actions like starting a timer, turning on Focus, or running a shortcut.
- Start a new search by pressing the Clear Text button in the search box.

**Turn off location-based suggestions:**

- Go to Settings > Privacy & Security > Location services.
- Tap System Services.
- Turn off "Suggestions and search" option.

**App Search:**

– Many apps have a search field or button to search for specific content within the app.

– In an app, tap the search box or Search button.

- If not available, swipe from top to bottom.

- Enter your search query and press Search.

**Add dictionary:**

- Go to Settings > General > Dictionary.

- Select a dictionary to add. By using Spotlight Search effectively, you can quickly locate and access the information you need on your iPhone.

# Manage Cellular Data Settings

To manage cellular data settings on your iPhone, follow these steps:

## Turn cellular data on or off:

- Go to Settings > Cellular.
- Turn the Cellular Data switch on or off.

## Adjust mobile data options:

- Go to Settings > Cellular > Mobile data options.
- To reduce mobile usage, turn on low data mode or tap Data mode

and select low data mode. This mode pauses automatic updates and background tasks when you're not connected to Wi-Fi.

- Turn data roaming on or off to allow Internet access over your mobile data network when you travel.

**Additional options depending on iPhone model and carrier:**

*1. Voice roaming (CDMA):*

- Turn this feature off to avoid being charged when using another carrier's network.

## 2. 4G/LTE Settings:

- Depending on your model and carrier, you may have options to enable or disable 4G/LTE or select Voice and Data (VoLTE) or Data only.

## 3. Smart data mode (5G models):

- Maximize battery life by selecting 5G Auto, which automatically switches to LTE when 5G speeds don't deliver better performance.

## 4. Allow more data on 5G:

- Enables higher quality HD video and FaceTime on 5G networks.

## 5. Set up personal hotspot:

- Go to Settings > Mobile network.

- Turn on mobile data, then tap Set up personal hotspot and follow the instructions.

**Manage mobile data usage for apps and services:**

- In Settings > Cellular, turn mobile data on or off for each app or service to control use their mobile data.
- Wi-Fi support is enabled by default and switches to mobile data if Wi-Fi connection is poor. Consider turning it off if you want to avoid using extra mobile data.

## SIM card lock:

- To prevent unauthorized use, you can lock the SIM card with a PIN code.

- Go to Settings > Mobile > SIM PIN and follow the prompts to set up a PIN for your SIM card.

# PERSONALIZE YOUR

# IPHONE

## Customize Sounds and Vibrations

To customize sounds and vibrations on your iPhone, follow these steps:

**Set sound and vibration preferences:**

1.  Open Settings and tap "Sounds & Haptics."

2.  Adjust the volume of all sounds by dragging the slider under "Ringtones & Alerts".

3. Tap "Ringtones" or "Text tones".

4. At the top of the Ringtone or Text Tones screen, tap "Haptic."

5. Select a tone from the available options. 6. Select a vibration pattern or tap "Create new vibration" to create your own custom vibration pattern.

**Customize sounds for each specific contact:**

1. Go to the Contacts application.

2. Tap the contact whose sound you want to personalize.

3. Click "Edit" in the upper right corner.

4. Select ringtones and message tones specific to this contact.

**Turn haptic feedback on or off:**

1. For supported models, go to Settings > Sound & Haptics.
2. Turn "System Haptics" on or off to enable or disable haptic feedback.
   - When turned off, you will not feel vibrations for incoming calls and alerts.

**Turn sound on and off:**

1. On iPhone 14 or later, go to Settings > Accessibility > Sound & Visual.

2. Enable "Sound on and off" so that iPhone makes a sound when turned on and off.

**Check Do Not Disturb settings:**

- If you're not receiving incoming calls and notifications as expected, open Control Center and make sure Do Not Disturb is not turned on. Tap the Do Not Disturb icon to turn it off if it is ticked.

# Customize and Use Action Buttons

To customize and use Action Buttons on iPhone 15 Pro and iPhone 15 Pro Max, follow these steps:

## Customize Action Buttons:

1. Open the Settings app on your iPhone.
2. Scroll down and tap "Action button".
3. You'll see a screen displaying icons representing actions that you can assign to the action button.
4. Swipe left or right to browse available actions until you find the one you want to use.

5. Tap the action you want to assign to the Action button.

## Available actions:

- Silent mode: Turn silent mode on or off.
- Focus: Enable or disable a specific focus mode.
- Camera: Quickly open the Camera app to take photos, selfies, videos, portraits or portrait selfies.
- Flashlight: Turn the flashlight on or off.

- Voice Memo: Start or stop recording a voice memo. - Magnifier: Open the Magnifier app.

- Translate: Start translating speech from one language to another.

- Shortcut: Open an app or run your favorite shortcut.

- Accessibility: Get quick access to your favorite accessibility features.

- No Action: Do nothing.

## Using the action button:

1. After customizing the action button, hold it.

2. The assigned action will be executed.

3. For functions like silent mode, pressing and holding the Action button again will toggle the setting on or off.

*By following these steps, you can customize the Action button on iPhone 15 Pro or iPhone 15 Pro Max to perform the functions you use most often, providing quick access to features and actions.*

# Manage Your iPhone Lock Screen

To create, customize, and manage your iPhone lock screen, including adding a wallpaper, changing fonts, and linking the lock screen to Foci, follow these steps:

1.  **New lock screen customization:**

    -   Touch and hold the lock screen until the "Customize" and "Add new" buttons appear at the bottom.

    -   Tap "Add new" to create a new lock screen, or swipe to the screen you want to change and tap "Customize," then tap "Lock screen. "

- Choose a background image from the options provided, or select "Photo" or "Shuffle Photo" to use your own image.
- Tap time to adjust font, color and style. - Add a widget by tapping "Add Widget" or tapping the date or field below the time.
- Once completed, tap "Add" or "Done", then select "Set as wallpaper pair" or "Personalize home screen".

## 2. Customize your photo on the lock screen:

- If you select a photo, you can reposition it by pinching it to zoom in or out and dragging with two fingers.
- Swipe left or right to try different photo styles with color filters and additional fonts.
- For photos that support overlays, tap "Add" and select "Depth effect" for a multi-layered effect.
- If you select Live Photo, press the Play button to preview the motion effect.
- Adjust the shuffle frequency if you select Shuffle Photos.

## 3. Assign focus to your lock screen:

- Touch and hold the lock screen until the "Personalize" button appears.

- Tap "Spotlight" at the bottom and select the Spotlight option, then tap "Close".

## 4. Edit or modify your lock screen:

- Follow steps 1 and 2 to further customize your lock screen.

## 5. Switch between lock screens:

- Touch and hold the lock screen until "Personalization" appears.

- Swipe to the lock screen you want

  to use and touch it.

## 6. Remove lock screen:

- Touch and hold the lock screen

  until "Personalization" appears.

- Swipe up on the lock screen you

  want to delete, tap the Trash

  button, then confirm by tapping

  "Delete this wallpaper".

*By following these steps, you can create,*

*customize, and manage your iPhone's*

*lock screen according to your preferences*

*and needs.*

# Change Wallpaper on iPhone

To change wallpaper on your iPhone:

## 1. Go to Wallpaper settings

- Go to Settings > Wallpaper, then tap Add new wallpaper.

## 2. Access wallpaper gallery

- Clicking on it will open the wallpaper gallery.

## 3. Choose a wallpaper option

- Tap the button at the top of the gallery (e. g. Photos, Mix Photos, Live Photos) to choose a template, such as a photo, emoji template, or local weather photo.

- You can also choose wallpaper from the provided sets such as Collection, Astronomy or Weather.

## 4. Additional personalization

- If you add a photo or random picture and want to personalize it, see Personalize your lock screen photo.
- Tap More and switch to one of the following options:
- Choose whether you want to use the wallpaper on both the lock screen and home screen by tapping Set as wallpaper pair.
- For additional Home screen changes, tap Customize Home

Screen. Adjust options like color, photo position, or add opacity for better app visibility.

# Adjust Screen Brightness, Color, And Display Settings

Controlling screen brightness and color on iPhone can improve your viewing experience and even extend the life of your iPhone battery. Here's how to manage these settings manually or automatically using various features like Dark Mode, True Tone, and Night Shift.

## Manually adjust screen brightness:

To manually adjust iPhone screen brightness, you can:

1. Open Control Center and slide the Brightness button up or down.

2. Go to Settings > Display & Brightness and adjust the brightness using the slider.

## Automatically adjust screen brightness:

iPhone can adjust screen brightness based on ambient light conditions:

1. Go to Settings > Accessibility.

2. Tap Display & text size, then turn on automatic brightness.

**Enable and configure Dark Mode:**

Dark Mode provides a darker color
palette suitable for low-light
environments:

1. To turn on Dark Mode, open Control
   Center, tap and hold the Brightness
   button, then tap Appearance. button.
2. You can also go to Settings > Display
   & Brightness and select Dark or Light
   mode.

**Set a dark schedule:**

Automatically activate dark mode at
night or according to a custom schedule:

1. In Settings > Display & brightness, turn on Auto and tap Options.

2. Select From Dusk to Dawn or set a custom schedule.

**Turn Night Shift on or off:**

Night Shift adjusts display colors for easier night viewing:

1. Open Control Center, hold down the Brightness button, then tap the Night Shift button.

2. To schedule Night Shift, go to Settings > Display & Brightness > Night Shift and adjust the settings accordingly.

**True Tone adjustment:**

True Tone adjusts display color based on ambient light:

1. In Control Center, touch and hold the Brightness button, then press the True Tone button to turn it on or off .

2. You can also go to Settings > Display & Brightness and turn on True Tone.

# Update Your iPhone Name

## Rename your iPhone

You have the option to rename your iPhone, this option is used in various functions like iCloud, AirDrop, Personal Hotspot core and interface with your computer.

1. Go to Settings > General > About > Name.
2. Tap the existing name to delete, enter the new name you want, then tap Done.

# Adjust Date and Time Settings

## Customize date and time

The date and time displayed on the lock screen are usually set automatically based on your current location. However, you can tailor them to your needs, especially when traveling.

1. Go to Settings > General > Date & Time.

2. Enable one of the following options:

   - Set automatically: Allows your iPhone to sync with the network time and adjust to your time zone. Note that not all networks support this feature. Therefore, manual

adjustment may be necessary in

some regions.

- 24-hour time: This setting displays

  the time in 24-hour format,

  displaying hours from 0 to 23.

*To change the default date and time*

*settings, turn off Set automatically and*

*do the following Adjust if necessary.*

# Change Language and Region Settings

## Adjust language and region

When you first set up iPhone, you choose your preferred language and region. However, if you travel or move, you can easily change these settings.

1. Go to Settings > General > Language & Region.

2. Customize as follows:

   - Language options for your iPhone.
   - Your preferred form of address (feminine, masculine or neutral).

Turn on "Share with all apps" for custom addressing across apps (available for some major languages like Spanish).

- Region settings.

- Calendar format.

- Temperature unit (Celsius or Fahrenheit).

- Metric system (metric, US or UK).

- First day of the week.

- Live Text function (allows you to select text in an image to copy or manipulate).

3. To add another language and keyboard, tap "Add language" and choose from the available options.

# Customize Home Screen on iPhone

## Create and manage folders

Organizing your apps into folders can streamline page navigation on your Home screen.

### 1. Create a folder:

– Press and hold the home screen wallpaper until the apps start to vibrate.

– Drag an app into another app to create a folder.

– Add additional applications to the folder if desired.

- You can have multiple application sites in a folder.

- To rename a folder, press and hold the folder, select "Rename" and enter a new name.

- If the app starts vibrating, tap the home screen background and try again.

## 2. Complete arrangement:

- When finished, tap "Done," then double-tap the Home screen background.

- To delete a folder, open it, drag all the apps to it and the folder will be automatically deleted.

*Note:* Arranging apps on the Home screen does not affect the arrangement of apps in the App Library.

## Move apps from folder to Home screen

Easily move apps from folder to Home screen for easier, faster access.

1. Navigate to the Home screen page that contains the folder containing the desired application.

2. Open the folder by clicking on it.

3. Press and hold the app until it starts vibrating.

4. Drag the app out of the folder onto the Home Screen.

**Managing Widgets on iPhone**

Widgets provide quick access to current information like weather updates, reminders, and interactive features like those found in Word Reminder and Family Utilities. They provide snapshots of important data, allowing users to stay informed without opening the application.

## Add widget to home screen

1. Go to the desired home screen page and long press on the background until the app starts to vibrate.
2. Tap the "Add widget" button at the top of the screen to open the widget library.
3. Scroll or search for the desired widget, select it, and scroll through the available size options.

4. Once you find your preferred size, tap "Add extension. "

5. While the apps are still vibrating, move the widget to the desired location, then tap "Done".

## Interact with widgets

Widgets on templates or The Home lock screen allows users to perform tasks without opening the corresponding app. For example, tapping an item in the Reminders widget will check it, or tapping the Play button in the Podcasts widget will start episode player

## Personalize your home screen widget

1. On the home screen, press and hold a widget to open the quick actions menu.

2. Select "Edit [widget name]" or "Edit stack" for Smart Stacks, then adjust the settings as desired.

3. For Smart Stacks, options include enabling smart rotation or widget suggestions, rearranging widgets, adding or removing them, and more.

4. Click "Done" to save changes.

## Remove widget from home screen

1. Press and hold the widget to open the quick action menu.

2. Tap "Remove widget" or "Remove stack," then confirm deletion.

## Show widgets in Today view

Access widgets in Today view by swiping right from the left edge of the Home screen and scrolling.

## Show widgets in Today View and Find when iPhone is locked

Allow access to Day View and Find from the lock screen:

1. Go to Settings > Face ID & Passcode (or Touch ID & Passcode).

2. Enter the passcode.

3. Toggle on "Today View and Search" under "Allow Access When Locked."

# Setting up Focus on iPhone

## Learn about Focus

Focus is a feature designed to minimize distractions and establish boundaries, allowing users to focus on specific activities. Users can choose from predefined Focus options like Work, Personal, or Sleep, or create a personalized Focus that suits their needs. Focus allows users to temporarily turn off all notifications or allow only relevant ones, letting others know that they are busy.

### Turn on Focus

1. Go to Settings > Focus on your iPhone.

2. Select a focus option like Do Not Disturb, Personal, Sleep, or Work.

3. Customize the selected Focus according to your preferences.

## Customize Focus options

- Specify which apps and contacts can send notifications during Focus.

- Adjust settings like showing silent notifications on the lock screen, dimming the lock screen, or hiding notification badges on home

screen apps.

- Customize the lock screen and

home screen page associated with

Focus to display relevant apps and

widgets.

## Focus filter added

- Improved focus settings by adding

an app filter to determine what

information is displayed during

focus.

- Choose which calendars, email

accounts, message conversations,

or specific Safari tab groups will be accessible in Focus.

## Create a custom focus

- If none of the predefined options meet your needs, create a custom focus.
- Go to Settings > Spotlight, tap the More button, select Customize, and set your Spotlight name, color, and icon.
- Customize focus options to your preferences.

## Sync focus across devices

- Ensure consistent focus settings across all Apple devices by enabling cross-device sharing in Settings > Focus.

## Activate or schedule Focus

- Activate Focus directly from the control center or schedule it to turn on automatically based on time, location or app usage.
- Configure options such as automatically replying to incoming notifications during Focus.

## Turn off or remove Focus

- Quickly turn off Focus to continue receiving notifications or use Siri commands to manage Focus settings.
- Remove unnecessary focus settings in Settings > Focus.

## Keep focused while driving

- Helps drivers concentrate more to minimize distractions on the road, ensuring safety.
- Customize automatic response settings and activation options based on driving conditions.

- Bypass driving announcements when you are a passenger to receive calls, texts and notifications.

*By using these features, users can effectively manage distractions and stay focused on their iPhone, whether while working, playing, or driving.*

# WORK WITH TEXT AND

# GRAPHICS

## Entering Text Using the On-Screen Keyboard

The On-Screen Keyboard on iPhone lets you enter and edit text efficiently.

### Text entry

1. Open any text editing application and tap the text field to activate the virtual keyboard.

2. Press each key to type or use QuickPath to move from letter to

letter without lifting your finger, allowing for seamless word creation. QuickPath may not be available in all languages.

3. Raise your finger to end a word. You can switch between input methods even in the middle of a sentence. (Note: Pressing the Delete key after using QuickPath will delete the entire word.)

## Keyboard functions

– Type capital letters by pressing the Shift key or touching and dragging the Shift key to a letter.

- Enable caps lock by pressing the Shift key twice.

- Quickly end sentences with periods and spaces by pressing the spacebar twice.

- Access numbers, punctuation, or symbols by pressing the Number or Symbol key.

- Cancel autocorrect by tapping the underlined word and selecting the desired spelling. - Correct spelling errors by tapping the misspelled word and choosing from suggested misspellings.

– Undo or redo the last edit by swiping left or right with three fingers, respectively.

**Keyboard Settings**

- Customize keyboard feedback by going to Settings > Sounds & Feeling > Keyboard Feedback.
- Turn on audio to hear typing sounds or Haptic to feel vibrations when typing.

**Touchpad mode**

- Turns the virtual keyboard into a touchpad to easily move the insertion point or select text.
- Touch and hold the spacebar until the keyboard turns light gray.
- Drag your finger on the keyboard to move the insertion point.
- Touch and hold with a second finger to select text and adjust the selection by moving the first finger.

**Enter accented characters**

- While typing, touch and hold a letter, number, or symbol related to the desired character.

- Drag and drop your finger on the option you want to enter.

## Move text

- In a text editor application, select the text you want to move.

- Touch and hold the selected text, then drag it to the desired location in the application.

- If you change your mind, lift your finger before dragging or dragging the text off the screen.

## Typing options

- Customize typing features like predictive typing and autocorrect by accessing keyboard settings.

- Access keyboard settings by pressing and holding the following keyboard's Emoji key or the Keyboard Switch key while typing, or go to Settings > General > Keyboard.

## One-handed typing

- Makes one-handed typing easier by adjusting the keyboard layout closer to your thumb.
- Press and hold the following keyboard's Emoji key or the Switch Keyboard key.
- Select a keyboard layout (e. g. right-handed layout) to reposition the keyboard accordingly.
- Tap the right or left edge of the keyboard to re-center it.

# Dictate text on iPhone

Dictation on iPhone lets you dictate text anywhere you can type. You can seamlessly switch between voice typing and touch typing, while still having access to the keyboard while dictating. This allows for easy integration of typing and dictation features, such as selecting text by touch and replacing with your voice.

## Availability and considerations

-   Dictation requests are processed locally on your device in multiple languages without an internet connection.

- Note that dictation capabilities may vary by language, region, and country, with functionality likely to vary.

## Enable dictation

1. Go to Settings > General > Keyboard.
2. Enable dictation. If prompted, confirm by tapping Enable dictation.
3. For more details about privacy and data sharing, tap About spelling and privacy.

## Using dictation

1. Open a text field and position the insertion point where you want to start dictating text.

2. Press the Dictation button on the virtual keyboard or in any text field if available.

3. Start dictating your text when the Dictation button appears near the insertion point.

4. To insert emoji, punctuation, or perform formatting tasks:

   - Mention the name of the emoji or punctuation (e. g. "heart emoji" or "exclamation mark").

   - Commands formatting such as "new line" or "new paragraph".

- *Note:* In supported languages, automatic dictation includes commas, periods, and question marks. To turn off automatic punctuation, go to Settings > General > Keyboard and turn off automatic punctuation.

5. Press the Dictation button again when finished. Dictation automatically stops after 30 seconds of silence.

6. You can also use the dictation feature in different languages if you configure multiple keyboards.

**Turn off dictation**

1. Go to Settings > General > Keyboard.

2. Turn off Enable Dictation to turn off the dictation feature.

## Use Predictive Text on iPhone

Predictive Text on iPhone streamlines your typing experience by suggesting words, emojis, and information as you write messages. These suggestions help you complete entire sentences with minimal effort. Here's how to take advantage of predictive text on your iPhone:

## Inline text predictions

- As you type, inline predictions to complete the word or phrase you're currently typing will appear. appears in gray text.

- Press the spacebar to accept the prediction or press repeatedly to reject it.
- If you accept a prediction but change your mind, press the Delete key, then tap the word you were entering to go back.

## Predictive suggestions

- Suggested words, emojis, and information appear above the virtual keyboard as you type.
- Tap a suggestion to apply it to your message.

- Note that accepting a suggested word automatically inserts a space after the word, while entering punctuation removes the space.
- To reject the suggestion, tap your original word or continue typing.

**Turn off predictive text**

- To turn off predictive text, press and hold the Next Keyboard key or the Emoji key or the Keyboard Switch key.
- Tap Keyboard Settings and turn off Prediction.

- Turning off Prediction also disables inline text prediction.

# Manage keyboards on iPhone

## Add or remove keyboards

1. Go to Settings > General > Keyboard.

2. Tap Keyboard.

3. To add a keyboard, tap Add new keyboard and select from the list. Repeat to add more.

4. To remove a keyboard, tap Edit, then tap the Delete button next to the keyboard you want to remove.

## Switch keyboards

- While typing, tap and hold Next Keyboard, Emoji, or Switch Keyboard.
- Select the desired keyboard from the list.

## Specify an alternative layout

1. Go to Settings > General > Keyboard > Keyboard.
2. Tap a language at the top, then choose a different layout from the list.

# Take a Screenshot on iPhone

## Take a screenshot using Face ID:

1. Quickly press and release the Side button and the Volume Up button at the same time.

2. Screenshot thumbnails appear briefly in the lower left corner of your screen.

3. Tap the thumbnail to see the screenshot or swipe left to hide it.

*Note: Screenshots are automatically saved to your library in the Photos app. To access, go to Photos > Album > Screenshots.*

## Take a screenshot using Touch ID:

1. Quickly press and release the Side button and the Home button at the same time.

2. Similar to Face ID, a screenshot thumbnail will briefly appear in the lower left corner.

3. Tap the thumbnail to view the screenshot or swipe left to hide.

*Note: Screenshots are automatically saved to your library in the Photos app. To access it, go to Photos > Album > Screenshots.*

## Full page screenshots:

- You can take screenshots of content that exceeds the length of your iPhone screen you, such as the entire website in Safari.

1. Follow the same steps as above depending on your device type (Face ID or Touch ID).

2. After tapping the screenshot thumbnail, select "Whole Page," then tap "Done."

3. Choose to save the screenshot directly to Photos or as a PDF file in the Files app.

*Note: Full-page screenshots are saved based on the specified location.*

# Record Screen Activity on iPhone

## Start Screen Recording:

1.  Go to Settings > Control Center and add the Screen Recording button to Control Center.

2.  Once added, open Control Center and tap the Screen Recording button.

3.  Wait for a 3-second countdown before starting recording.

## Stop screen recording:

-   To finish recording, open Control Center again and tap the Screen

Recording button or the red status bar at the top of the screen.

- Then press "Stop" to end recording.

**Access screen recordings:**

- Screen recordings are automatically saved to your camera roll in the Photos app.
- To locate them, go to Photos > Albums > Screen Recordings.

# Use Markups to Enhance Documents

### Use markup tools:

In supported apps like Mail, Messages, Notes, and Photos, markup tools for allows you to add drawings and sketches to your documents. You can also use markup to annotate screenshots, PDF files, and more.

1. Open a supported app and tap the Comments button or the Comments option.

2. Choose a writing tool such as a pen, highlighter, or pencil from the Annotation toolbar.

3. Use your finger to write or draw directly on the document.

4. While drawing, you can adjust various settings:

    - Change line thickness by selecting the drawing tool and pressing an option.

    - Adjust opacity by selecting the drawing tool and dragging the slider.

    - Change color by pressing the Color Picker button and choosing from Grid, Spectrum, or Slider.

5. To draw a straight line, select the Ruler tool, draw along the edge of the

ruler, and adjust the angle or position as needed.

6. Close the Annotate toolbar by pressing the Annotate or Done button when finished.

**Erase error:**

- If you make a mistake, use the Eraser tool on the Annotation toolbar.

- Tap the Eraser tool and choose between Pixel Eraser or Object Eraser.

- To erase, use your finger to rub the error or touch the object directly.

## Move marked object:

1. Select the Lasso tool from the Annotation toolbar.

2. Drag your finger to circle the items you want to move.

3. Lift your finger and drag the selected items to a new location.

4. Tap the screen to exit the Lasso tool mode.

*Note:* If the Annotations toolbar is not visible, tap the Annotations button or the Annotations option to access it. If it's minimized, tap its minimized version to enlarge it.

## Add text, shapes, signatures, and more:

In various supported apps, markup tools provide the ability to Flexible capabilities to embed text, shapes, signatures, stickers and image descriptions into your documents and images.

## Text added:

1. Open a supported app and navigate to the bookmarks section.

2. Click the Add button on the Annotation toolbar and select Add Text.

3. Enter your text using the keyboard.

4. Customize font, size, style, alignment, and color as needed.

5. Manage text boxes with the Add button.

6. Tap outside the text box to finish.

**Add shape:**

1. Access markup in supported apps.

2. Click the Add button and select Add shape.

3. Select the desired shape and adjust its properties.

4. Resize, move or modify the shape if necessary.

5. Additional options are available via the Add button.

6. Complete the settings by touching the screen.

**Drawing:**

1. In a supported application, navigate to Markup.

2. Select the writing tool from the Annotation toolbar.

3. Draw a shape with a single stroke to automatically create a perfect version.

4. There are many different shapes, including lines, arcs, squares, circles, etc.

5. Customize design according to needs.

## Signature added:

1. Access bookmarks in supported apps.

2. Click the Add button and select Add Signature.

3. Sign with your finger and adjust its position and properties.

4. Further changes can be made via the Add button.

5. Complete installation and exit.

## Managing signatures:

1. After creating a signature, navigate to the markup section.

2. Click the Add button and select Add signature.

3. Select Add or Remove Signature to manage existing signatures.

4. Create a new signature or delete an existing signature if necessary.

## Add stickers:

1. Access bookmarks in supported apps.

2. Tap the Add button and select Add sticker.

3. Drag and drop the sticker onto your document or photo.

4. Adjust angle and size as desired.

## Add custom image description:

1. Access markup in supported apps like Photos.

2. Press the Add button and select Description.

3. Enter your description and complete.

*These markup features let you*

*personalize and enrich your documents*

*and images directly from iPhone.*

# Fill Out Forms and Add Signatures on iPhone

## Fill Out Forms and Sign Documents:

1. Open the document by tapping it.

2. If prompted, use the Files app to open and save the document.

3. Tap the AutoFill button and enter text in the blank fields using the on-screen keyboard.

4. To fill in additional fields, tap them and enter the required text.

5. Add additional text or your signature by pressing the Add button and selecting:

- Add a text template box: Drag and position the text box, then enter the text.
- Add signature: Sign with your finger and place it in the document.

6. Once completed, tap the Share button to send the document via Mail, Messages, or AirDrop.

7. Click Done to close the document.

**Use autocompletes to fill out a form:**

1. Open the document by tapping it.

2. If prompted, use the Files app to open and save the document.

3. Press the AutoFill button and select a blank field.

4. Select from your saved contact information to automatically fill in the field.

5. If desired, select "Select another" to enter another contact's details.

6. Tap any field to make adjustments using the on-screen keyboard.

7. Click Done to complete and close the document.

*These methods simplify the process of filling out forms and signing documents right on your iPhone, improving efficiency and convenience.*

# Exploring Visual Look Up for Image Identification on iPhone

Visual Look Up empowers you to recognize and explore various elements within your photos and videos directly in the Photos app. Through Visual Look Up, you can discover details about famous landmarks, plants, pets, and more. Additionally, it can even identify food items in photos and suggest related recipes.

**Here's how to use Visual Look Up:**

1. Open a photo in full screen or pause a video at any frame within the Photos app.

2. Find the Display Info button at the bottom of the screen. If it has a star icon, such as the Detected Food Info button or the Detected Dog Info button, visual search is available.

3. Press the Track Info button to access detailed information.

4. Next, tap "Search" at the top of the photo information to display visual search results.

5. To exit the visual search results, press the Close button. You can also swipe

down on the photo or video frame to

close the photo information.


*Please note that visual search may vary*

*depending on your device model and is*

*not available in all regions or languages.*

# Applications on

# iPhone

## App Store

### Get apps from the App Store on iPhone

In the App Store app, you can explore a variety of apps, featured stories, tips and tricks, and in-app events.

*Note:* To use the App Store, you need an internet connection and an Apple ID. Availability on the App Store and Apple Arcade may vary by country or region.

**Discover apps:**

- Today: Discover selected stories, apps and events in the app.
- Games: Find your next gaming adventure across numerous categories such as action, adventure, racing, puzzle and more.
- Apps: Browse new releases, top lists or search by category.
- Arcade: Immerse yourself in a curated collection of premium Apple Arcade games (subscription

required), without ads or in-app purchases.

- Search: Enter what you're looking for, then tap Search on the keyboard. You can also explore different categories or view suggested apps. Learn more about an app:

Tap an app to view details such as screenshots or previews, in-app events, ratings and reviews, supported languages, compatibility with other Apple devices, file size, and privacy information.

**Download an app:**

Tap Get (for free apps) or price. If you see the "Redownload" button, it means you have already purchased the app. Tap it to download it again for free. If necessary, authenticate yourself with Face ID, Touch ID or your password.

**Access the App Store widget:**

View in-app stories, collections and events right on your home screen. Learn how to add, edit and delete widgets on iPhone.

**Share or gift an app:**

Tap the app, then tap the share button.
Choose a sharing option or tap Gift App
(not available for all apps).

**Redeem or send an Apple Gift
Card:**

Click My Account or your photo in the
top right corner. Then tap Redeem Gift
Card or Code or Send Gift Card via Email.

**Discover games from the App Store
on iPhone**

Discover a wide range of games in the App Store app in various categories, including action, adventure, racing, puzzles and more.

*Note: Game Center, Apple Arcade and Apple One availability may vary.*

**Search games:**

- Games: Browse new releases, top lists or search by category.
- Arcade: Enjoy a collection of premium Apple Arcade games (subscription required) without ads or in-app purchases.

- Search: Tap the search bar, enter your search query, then tap Search on the keyboard.

**Learn more about a game:**

Tap a game to view details such as screenshots or previews, in-app events, ratings and reviews, supported languages, compatibility with other Apple devices, file size, and privacy information.

**Download a game:**

Press the price. For free games, tap Get. If you see the "Redownload" button, it means you have already purchased the game. Tap it to download it again for free. If necessary, authenticate yourself with Face ID, Touch ID or your password.

**Connect a game controller to your iPhone:**

Pair a Bluetooth game controller or connect one via the Lightning or USB-C port. Customize the button layout and even add a second controller for cooperative play.

To pair Bluetooth, follow the instructions on the remote control and go to Settings >

Bluetooth on your iPhone. For Lightning

or USB-C connections, use a compatible

controller and necessary adapters.

Customize the button layout in Settings >

General > Game Controllers. Use the

buddy controller feature to combine two

controllers for cooperative gameplay.

# Books

## Buy books and audiobooks on iPhone

In the Books app, explore bestsellers, chart-toppers, series, and recent lists curated by Apple Books editors. Once you select a book or audiobook, you can read or listen to it directly in the Books app.

### Search and buy:

1. Open the Books app on your iPhone.
2. Tap Bookstore or Audiobooks to search for titles, or use Search to find a specific title, author, series, or genre.

- *Tip: Tap Browse Sections to view titles in categories like Charts and Book Clubs, or genres like Biographies & Memoirs and Young Adults.*

3. Tap a book cover to view more details, read a sample, listen to a preview, or mark it as Read.

4. Tap "Buy" to purchase a title or "Get" to download a free title.

*All purchases are made using the payment method associated with your Apple ID.*

**Manage downloads:**

- Enable automatic downloads of books and audiobooks over your mobile network by Go to Settings > Books. Then enable "Automatic Downloads". Choose your preferred download settings.

**Annotate books:**

- Highlight, underline, and take notes while reading books in the Books app. Share your notes with others.
- To highlight or underline text, touch and hold a word, then adjust the selection and touch Highlight.

Adjust highlight colors or switch to underline. Remove any highlighting or underlining if necessary.

- Add notes by tapping and holding a word and then selecting Add Note. Enter your text and tap Done. Delete notes or view all your notes in bookmarks and highlights.

**Share highlights and notes:**

- Open a book where you have saved highlights or notes. Tap any page, then tap the menu button >

Bookmarks and Highlights >
Highlights.

- Touch and hold the highlight or
note you want to share, then tap
Share. Choose a sharing method
such as AirDrop, Messages or
Mail.

**Listen to audiobooks:**

- Use the Books app to listen to
audiobooks on your iPhone.
- Tap Home, Library, or Search to
search for an audiobook. Tap the
cover art to start playing.

- During playback, you can fast forward or rewind, adjust volume, change playback speed, set a sleep timer, and more.

- Some audiobooks have PDF files attached, which you can find by tapping Learn More under the audiobook cover in your library and selecting View PDF Contents.

# Calculator

## Use Calculator on iPhone

In the Calculator app, you can easily perform basic arithmetic calculations using the standard calculator. Additionally, you can use the scientific calculator for advanced functions such as exponential, logarithmic and trigonometric calculations.

### Access Calculator:

- Open the Calculator application on your iPhone.

**Perform calculations:**

- For basic arithmetic calculations, use the standard calculator.

- For exponential, logarithmic and trigonometric functions switch to the scientific calculator.

**Use Siri:**

- Enable Siri and ask questions like "What is 74 times 9?" or "What is 18 percent of 225?" for hands-free calculations.

**Scientific Calculator:**

1. Rotate your iPhone to landscape mode.

2. Access the scientific calculator with advanced features.

## Copy, delete or erase numbers:

*- Copy calculation result:* Touch and hold the calculation result on the screen, then touch Copy. Paste the result somewhere else, such as a note or message.

*- Clear Last Digit:* If you make a mistake while entering a number, swipe left or right at the top of the screen to delete the last digit.

- *Clear Screen:* Tap the Clear button (C) to delete the last entry or tap the Clear All button (AC) to delete all entries at once.

# Calendar

## Create and edit calendar events on iPhone

The iPhone Calendar app is a powerful tool for managing your schedule. Here's how to create and edit events:

### Create an event:

1. ***Navigate to Day view:*** Open the Calendar app and navigate to Day view day.

2. ***Tap the Add button:*** At the top of the screen, tap the Add (+) button.

**3. Enter event details:** Fill in event details such as title, location, start and end time, guests, and attachments.

**4. Click Add:** After entering all necessary information, click Add to save the event.

## Notifications added:

- After creating an event, you can set up a reminder by tapping the event, selecting Edit, then tapping Alerts. Choose when you want to be called back.

## Add attachment:

- To attach a file to an event, tap Edit on the event details screen, then tap Add Attachment. Browse and select the file you want to attach.

**Copy and paste events:**

- Touch and hold the event you want to copy then tap Copy. Navigate to the date you want to paste the event, touch and hold for the desired amount of time, then tap Insert.

**Edit event:**

- Tap the event you want to edit, then tap Edit. Adjust the required fields and tap Done to save your changes.

## Delete Event:

- In Day View, tap the event you want to delete, then tap Delete Event at the bottom of the screen.

## Send invitation:

- Tap the event, tap Edit, then tap Guests. Add a contact or email

address, then tap Done to send the
invitation.

## Reply to an invitation:

- Respond to an event invitation by
  tapping the invitation in the
  Calendar app or inbox, then
  choosing Accept, Maybe, or
  Decline.

## Set up multiple calendars:

- Tap Calendars at the bottom of the
  screen, then tap Add Calendar to

create additional calendars for

different events.


**Subscribe to an external calendar:**

- Tap Add Subscription and enter

  the URL of the. iOS file to

  subscribe to the external calendar.


**Change calendar settings:**

- Personalize your calendar by

  changing colors, turning on event

  notifications, or unsubscribing

  from unwanted calendars.

**Manage Calendar accounts:**

- Manage calendar accounts in
  Settings > Calendar > Accounts.
  Add, remove, or customize
  accounts as needed.

**Move events between calendars:**

- Change the calendar for an event
  by tapping the event, selecting
  Calendars, and selecting the
  desired calendar.

# Camera

## iPhone Camera Basics

The Camera app on your iPhone offers different modes and features for taking photos and videos. Here's how to use it effectively:

### Open Camera:

*You can open the Camera app in many ways:*

- Tap the Camera icon on the welcome screen.
- Swipe left on the lock screen.

- Press and hold the Camera button on the lock screen.

- Open Control Center and tap the Camera button.

- Use Siri by saying "Open camera".

**Take a photo:**

- Open the camera and press the shutter button or press one of the volume buttons to take a photo.

- You can also swipe left or right to switch between different camera modes like Photo, Video, Cinema, Panorama and Portrait.

**Change camera mode:**

- Swipe left or right to switch between different camera modes.

- Choose from modes like Photo, Video, Time Lapse, Slow Motion, Panorama, Portrait, and more.

- Each mode offers distinct features for recording different types of content.

**Zoom in or out:**

- Pinch the screen to zoom in or out.

- On models equipped with dual or triple camera systems, switch

between different zoom levels for
more precise control.

## Video recording:

- Select video recording mode and
  press the Record button to start
  recording.
- While recording, you can press the
  Record button to capture a still
  image. - Pinch the screen to zoom
  in or out while recording video.
- Adjust video settings in Settings >
  Camera > Video recording.

## QuickTake Videos:

- In Photo mode, touch and hold the Shutter button to start recording a QuickTake video.

- Slide the shutter button to the right to lock for hands-free recording.

- Swipe up to zoom in or pinch to zoom out while recording.

**Slo-mo and fast motion video:**

- Select Slo-mo mode to record slow motion video.

- Select Time-lapse mode to capture scenes over a period of time.

- Adjust settings for these modes in Settings > Camera.

## Cinematic videos:

- Use cinematic mode to apply a depth of field effect to your videos.
- Tap to focus on various subjects while recording.
- Adjust cinematic mode settings in the camera.

## Scan Live Text & QR Code:

- Use Live Text to copy, share, search or translate text in the camera frame.
- Scan QR codes directly from the Camera app or use the code scanner in Control Center.

**Camera settings:**

- Customize camera settings in the Settings app in Camera.
- Adjust video recording format, enable Action mode, change slow motion settings, etc.

*By mastering these basics, you'll be able to take full advantage of your iPhone's camera and capture stunning photos and videos with ease.*

# Clock

## See the time worldwide in Clock on iPhone

With the Clock app on iPhone, you can easily see the time in different time zones around the world. Here's how:

1. **Open the Watch app:**

   - Locate and tap the Watch app icon on your iPhone's Home screen.

2. **Access World Clock:**

   - Tap the "World Clock" tab at the bottom of the screen.

## 3. City management:

- To add a city: Press the "+" (Add) button, then select the city from the list.

- To delete a city: Press "Edit", then press the red "x" (Delete) button next to the city you want to delete.

- To reorder cities: Tap "Edit", then use the ≡ (Reorder) button on the right to drag and reorder cities as desired.

## 4. Save changes:

- Once you're done managing your city list, tap "Done" in the upper right corner to save your changes.

**Set an alarm in Clock on iPhone:**

You can also use the Clock app to set alarms for different times of day. Here's how:

1. **Open the Watch app:**

   - Launch the Watch app on your iPhone.

2. **Alarm access:**

   - Tap the "Alarms" tab at the bottom of the screen.

## 3. Add alarm:

- Press the "+" (Add) button to create a new alarm.

## 4. Set alarm details:

- Select desired alarm time. - Select the days of the week when the alarm will repeat, if needed.

- Attach warning labels for easy identification.

- Select alarm sound.

- Turn on the switch to repeat if you want to enable it.

- Click "Save" to save the alarm.

## 5. Manage alarms:

- To edit an existing alarm, tap the alarm time or tap "Edit", then select the alarm you want to edit.
- To turn off the alarm, tap the switch next to the alarm time.
- To delete an alarm, swipe the alarm to the left, then tap "Delete".

*By following these steps, you can easily check the time in different cities around the world and set alarms to stay organized and on time.*

# Compass

## Use Compass on iPhone

The Compass app on iPhone can help you determine the direction you're heading, your current location, and your altitude. Here's how to use it:

1. **Open the Compass app:**

   - Locate and tap the Compass app icon on your iPhone home screen.

2. **Show Direction, Location, and Altitude:**

- The Compass screen will show the direction your iPhone is pointing, your current location, and the altitude.

- Your bearing, coordinates and altitude are displayed at the bottom of the screen.

## 3. Accuracy guaranteed:

- For accurate bearings, hold your iPhone flat to align the crosshair with the center of the compass.

- You can touch the compass dial to lock in your current direction.

## 4. Check your location in Maps:

- If you want to open your location in Maps, tap the coordinates shown at the bottom of the screen.

## 5. Allow location access for Compass:

- If the Compass app doesn't see your location, make sure location services are turned on:

- Go to Settings > Privacy and security > Location services.

- Enable location services if they are not already enabled.

- Scroll down and tap Compass.

- Select "When using the app" to
allow Compass to access your
location only when you are using
the app.

## 6. Note on accuracy:

- Remember that compass accuracy
can be affected by magnetic or
environmental interference.
- Avoid relying solely on a digital
compass for accurate navigation,
especially in areas likely to be
subject to magnetic interference.

*By following these steps, you can effectively use the Compass app on your iPhone to get direction, see your location, and check altitude if needed.*

# Contact

## Add and use contact information on iPhone

1. **Create a contact:**

   - Open the Contacts app on your iPhone.

   - Press the "+" or "Add" button.

   - Enter contact information such as name, phone number, email, etc.

   - Optionally, assign contacts to a specific group or account.

   - Click "Done" to save the contact.

2. **Find contact:**

   - Open the Contacts app.

- Tap the search box at the top.

- Enter name, address, phone number or other contact information.

- Contacts that match your search criteria will be displayed.

## 3. Share contacts:

- Open the Contacts app and select the contact you want to share.

- Tap a contact to view their contact details.

- Scroll down and tap "Share contact. "

- Choose how to send contact
  information (e. g. Message, Mail,
  AirDrop).
- All contact information will be
  shared.

## 4. Quick contact:

- In the Contacts app, select the
  contact you want to contact.
- Below the contact name, you'll find
  options to start a message, make a
  phone call, start a FaceTime call,
  compose an email, or send money
  with Apple Pay.

- Press the corresponding button to quickly contact the contact using the selected method.

## 5. Change default contact method:

If you want to change the default phone number or email address to contact a person:

- Press and hold the information method button desired contact (e. g. phone calls, emails).
- Select your preferred option from the list that appears.

## 6. Delete contact:

- Open the Contacts app and find the contact you want to delete.

- Tap a contact to see their contact details.

- Tap "Edit" in the upper right corner.

- Scroll down and tap "Delete contact".

- Confirm deletion when prompted.

# Facetime

## Get started with FaceTime on iPhone

**1. Set up FaceTime:**

- Go to Settings > FaceTime.

- Enable FaceTime if it is not already enabled.

- Enter your Apple ID or phone number in the "You can be reached by FaceTime at" section.

**2. Make a FaceTime call:**

- Open the FaceTime app.

- Tap "New FaceTime".

- Enter the name or phone number of the person you want to call.

- Press the FaceTime button to make a video call or the Call button to make an audio call.

## 3. Use FaceTime controls:

- During a call, use FaceTime controls to manage your speaker, camera, microphone, and more.

- Tap your screen to access controls if they are not visible.

## 4. Watch, listen and play together:

- Tap the "Share content" button during the call to share music, videos or exercises with other participants.

## 5. Record a video message:

- If someone doesn't answer your FaceTime call, tap "Record video" to leave a video message.
- Send your recorded message after recording is complete.

## 6. Receive a FaceTime call:

- Answer an incoming FaceTime call by dragging the slider or tapping "Accept".

- Reject the call by pressing "Reject" or "Leave call". "

- Set a reminder or send a message if you can't answer the call right away.

## 7. Create a FaceTime link:

- In the FaceTime app, tap "Create link" to create a link for FaceTime calling.

- Share link via Messages, Mail or other platforms to invite people to join the call.

## 8. Change your look:

- During calls, use Memoji, filters, text labels, stickers, and shapes to personalize your look.
- Press the Effects button to access these features.

## 9. Block unwanted callers:

- Block unwanted FaceTime calls by tapping "Block callers" in your call history or during a call.

- Mute FaceTime calls from
  unknown numbers by turning on
  "Mute Unknown Callers" in
  Settings > FaceTime.

## 10.  Report unwanted calls:

- Report unwanted FaceTime calls
  as spam by tapping "Block callers",
  then tap "Block and report
  unwanted calls " in your call
  history.

# Files

## Edit files, folders, and downloads in Files on iPhone

**1. Edit and reorganize documents:**

- Open supported document formats in the app File.

- Tap the page number in the upper left corner.

- Press the "Add" button.

- Select options such as Rotate Left/Right, Insert Blank Page, Insert from File, Scan Page or Delete.

- To rearrange pages, touch and hold a page, then drag it to a new location.

- Press the "Show inking tools" button to annotate the document.

## 2. Change view:

- In an open location or folder, press the "Add" button.

- Select List or Icon to switch between list view and icon view.

## 3. Rearrange the Browse screen:

- Tap the "More" button at the top of the Browse screen.

- Click "Edit".

- Hide location by disabling it.

- Delete a tag by pressing "Delete" next to the tag.

- Remove an item from Favorites by tapping "Delete".

- Change the order of an item by pressing and holding the Reorder button, then dragging the item to a new location.

## 4. Set up iCloud Drive:

- Go to Settings > [your name] > iCloud.

- Activate iCloud Drive.

## 5. Browse iCloud Drive:

- Open the Files app.

- Click "Browse" at the bottom.

- Tap iCloud Drive under Locations.

- Open folders by clicking on them.

## 6. Select Apps for iCloud Drive:

- In Settings > [your name] > iCloud.

- Enable or disable individual app access to iCloud Drive.

*By following these steps, you can effectively edit and reorganize files, folders, and downloads using the Files*

*app on iPhone. Additionally, you can*

*manage iCloud Drive settings and choose*

*which apps can access it.*

# Find My

## Share your location in Find My on iPhone:

1. **Set up location sharing:**

   - Open the Find My app.

   - Tap "Me" at the bottom.

   - Turn on "Share my location".

   - Optional, select "Use this iPhone as location. "

2. **Set a label for your location:**

   - Tap "Me" > "Locations".

   - Choose a label or add a custom label.

## 3. Share location with your friends:

- Click the Add button. - Select "Share my location".

- Enter a friend's name or select a contact.

- Press "Send" and select duration.

## 4. Stop sharing your location:

- To stop sharing with friends, tap "Everyone," then tap the friend's name and select "Stop sharing location my mind. "

- To hide your location from everyone, go to "Me" and turn off "Share my location".

## Find friends in Find My on iPhone

### 1. See a Friend's location:

- Tap "People", then tap the friend's name.
- If available, their location will be shown on the map.

### 2. Contact a friend:

- Tap "Contact" under the friend's name and select a contact method.

### 3. Get directions for friends:

- Tap "Directions" under your friend's name to open Maps.

### 4. Label your friend's location:

- Tap your friend's name.
- Tap "Edit location name" and select a label or add a custom label.

### 5. Mark your favorite friends:

- Click on your friend's name and add them to Favorites for quick access.

## Add your iPhone to Find My

### 1. Add your iPhone:

- Go to Settings > [your name] > Find My.

- Activate "Find my iPhone".

### 2. Additional settings:

- Option to enable "Find my network" and "Send last location".

## Find a device in Find My on iPhone

### 1. See a device's location:

- Tap "Devices" and select the device

  you want to locate.

- If present, its location will be

  indicated on the map.

## 2. Play sound on device:

- Tap the device then tap "Play

  sound".

## 3. Get directions to your device:

- Tap the device then tap

  "Directions" to open Maps.

## Adjust map settings in Find My on iPhone

### 1. Change map view:

- Tap the button at the top right of the map and select the map type.

– You can optionally click the Add button for further customization.

### 2. Change distance units:

- Adjust default distance units in iPhone settings.

# Fitness

## Start your fitness journey with iPhone

Start your fitness journey with the Fitness app on iPhone. Whether you're looking to achieve specific fitness goals or just want to stay active, the Fitness app offers comprehensive tools to track your progress, recommend completed workouts achieve and share your achievements with others. Additionally, by subscribing to Apple Fitness+, you get access to a variety of guided workouts and meditations to support you on your wellness journey.

## Track your daily activity

Open the Fitness app and go to the Activity area to track your daily activity. Track your movement counts, track steps taken, set personalized movement goals, and see your progress over time. With the inclusion of a Move Ring, Exercise Ring (for quick activities), and Stand Ring (for hourly movements), Apple Watch users can comprehensively track their daily physical activity.

## Check your trends

Get insights into your fitness journey by reviewing trends in the Fitness app. Evaluate your progress over the past 90 days compared to last year, providing valuable feedback on your fitness efforts.

## Share your activity with friends

Share your fitness journey with friends and family by accessing the sharing feature in the Fitness app. Invite friends to join you on your fitness journey, see their highlights, and get notifications when they reach their goals or complete their workouts.

## Get active with Apple Fitness plus

Explore the range of workouts available through Apple Fitness+, designed to suit all fitness levels. From cycling and strength training to yoga and treadmill workouts, Apple Fitness+ offers a variety of options to fit your preferences and goals. Just tap Fitness+ to start your journey to a healthier lifestyle.

## Track your daily activity and change your goals

Use the Fitness app to track your daily activity and adjust your exercise goals if necessary. Even without an Apple Watch, users can still track their progress and

observe their movement trends over time.

## Subscribe to Apple Fitness+

 Unleash the full potential of your fitness

journey by subscribing to Apple Fitness+.

Access a massive library of guided

workouts and meditations, complete with

on-screen instructions and personalized

metrics to enhance your workout

experience.

## Start a workout or meditation

Start a workout or meditation directly from your iPhone in the Fitness app. Choose your preferred activity type, preview available options, and easily start your session. Enjoy the flexibility to pause, resume, or stream your workouts to compatible devices for added convenience.

## Download exercises and meditations for offline use

Download your favorite exercises and meditations to iPhone for access Seamless offline. Stick to your fitness routine wherever you are, even without an Internet connection.

*With these features and functions, the iPhone Fitness app is the ultimate companion to help you achieve your fitness goals and promote a healthier lifestyle.*

# Freeform

## Explore Freeform on iPhone

Get creative with the Freeform app on iPhone, which offers an unlimited canvas for bringing together diverse elements like photos, drawings, links, and files. Collaborate with others easily and turn your ideas into reality.

### Gather ideas freely

Freeform boards, similar to online whiteboards, give you the freedom to combine any type of file without constraints on layout or page size. Just tap the New Board button to start your creative journey.

## Collaborate with others

Enable real-time collaboration by inviting others to work together on the Freeform panel. Use sticky notes for brainstorming sessions or feedback exchanges, promoting smooth teamwork.

## Get creative with drawing tools

Unleash your artistic side with the Freeform app's drawing and inking tools. Customize line weight, transparency, color, etc. to create impressive visual works.

## Seamless integration across devices

Start your work on iPhone and move seamlessly to your iPad or Mac, because Freeform panels stored in iCloud automatically sync across all your Apple devices. Turn on iCloud integration in Settings to take advantage of this feature.

## Create a freeform board on iPhone

Jumpstart your creativity by creating a board suitable for brainstorming and collaboration right from your iPhone. Choose from a variety of options like sticky notes, text boxes, designs, shapes, and images to create your boards with ease.

## Access and manage boards

Easily access and manage your Freeform boards on iPhone, whether opening recent boards, marking favorites, or accepting collaboration invitations. Customize the board's appearance and organization to your preferences.

## Draw and handwrite on the Freeform board

Express yourself freely by drawing or taking notes directly on the Freeform board with your finger. Explore a wide range of drawing tools and editing options to enhance your designs.

*With Freeform on iPhone, creativity has no limits. Immerse yourself in a world of endless possibilities and turn your ideas into tangible expressions of art and collaboration.*

# Health

## Get Started with Health on iPhone

The Health app on iPhone acts as a centralized hub to store and manage your health data from a variety of sources, including your device. you, Apple Watch, and compatible apps and devices. Learn how to organize your health information, set medication schedules, track your menstrual cycle, share data securely, and more.

### Access your health data

Easily access and manage your health data from one place. iPhone automatically collects and analyzes important health information, such as activity, sleep history, and even medical records from healthcare providers. Additionally, you can manually add information about medications, menstrual cycles, and more.

## Medication Management

Keep track of your medications by creating a complete list, scheduling your medications, and recording when you take them. Just go to the Medication section of the Health app, tap "Add Medication" and follow the prompts to enter relevant details.

## Menstrual cycle tracker

Use a cycle tracker to track your menstrual cycle, record symptoms, and predict your next period or fertile window Friend. Set up cycle tracking by tapping "Cycle Tracking" in the Browse section of the app and following the setup instructions.

## Secure data sharing

Share your health data securely with people you trust, including family, doctors and caregivers. You have complete control over what information to share, who to share it with, and when to stop sharing. Go to in-app Sharing to manage data sharing preferences.

## Monitor walking stability

iPhone can evaluate your walking stability using a custom algorithm, providing notifications if your stability gets low. You can also share these notifications with a trusted contact and access exercises to improve walking stability.

## Record your mood

Reflect on your mental health by recording momentary emotions and daily moods. Track the correlation between your mental state and lifestyle factors like exercise, sleep and daylight exposure.

## Take a mental health assessment

Take a standard mental health assessment in the Health app to assess your risk for depression or anxiety. These reviews can help you understand when to seek professional help.

## Set a sleep-focused schedule

Establish healthy sleep habits by creating regular bedtimes and wake-up times. Customize your Sleep Focus settings to minimize distractions before bed and ensure a restful sleep environment.

## Register as an organ donor

In the US, register as an organ, eye or tissue donor through Donate Life America directly from the Health app. Update your sponsor information or delete your registration if necessary.

## Easy to stay healthy

With the Health app on iPhone, managing your health and well-being is simpler and more convenient. Take advantage of its comprehensive features to stay organized, informed, and proactive about your health.

# Home

The Home app on iPhone provides a convenient and secure way to control and automate smart devices in your home, including lights, locks, thermostats, and more. Here's a guide to getting started with Home on your iPhone:

## Overview of Home

### 1. Categories:

Accessories are organized into categories such as Air Conditioners, Lights, Security, Speakers & TV or Water, which makes it easy to find and control them.

## 2. Camera:

See video feeds from up to four cameras directly in the Home app, with the ability to swipe left to see more cameras.

## 3. Scenes:

Create scenes to control multiple accessories with just a touch or Siri command, such as turning off lights and closing curtains at night.

## 4. Favorites:

Add frequently used accessories to Favorites for quick access from the Home tab.

## 5. *Room:*

Accessories are grouped by room, helping you effectively manage devices in your home.

## Edit Home tab:

- Reorder items, rearrange sections, or resize icons to customize the Home tab layout to your preferences.

**Upgrade to new home architecture:**

- iOS 16. 2 introduces a new, more
  reliable home architecture. Follow
  the steps to upgrade your home
  and make sure all connected
  devices are using the latest
  software.

**Control your home with Siri:**

- Use Siri voice commands to easily
  control your accessories and
  scenes.

## Control your home remotely:

- Allows remote control of your accessories from anywhere using a home hub device like Apple TV or HomePod.

## Set up security cameras:

- Use the Home app to view video activity recorded by cameras in your home, with additional features available for HomeKit security video cameras.

## Unlock your door with your house key:

- Some lock manufacturers offer the ability to unlock your door with your house key saved in Apple Wallet on your iPhone or Apple Watch. Set up and manage the Home key directly in the Home app.

## Set up a guest passcode:

- Grant temporary access to your home by setting up a guest passcode directly in the Home app.

## Add another home:

- If you have multiple physical spaces, like a home and a small office, you can add and manage them separately in the Home app.

# iTunes store

To download music, movies, and TV shows from the iTunes Store on your iPhone, follow these steps:

## Search for content:

### 1. *Browse categories:*

Open the iTunes app Store and go to Music, Movies or TV shows. You can browse by category and refine your search by tapping Categories.

### 2. *Check the Chart:*

Find out what's currently popular on iTunes by checking the Chart section.

### 3. Search:

Use the search function to search for specific songs, movies or TV shows by entering keywords.

### 4. Recommended:

Explore new content based on your previous purchases by tapping the "More" option.

### View and interact:

### 1. *Content Preview:*

Tap an item to see more detailed information about it. You can preview songs, watch movie and TV show trailers, or share the item with others.

### 2. *Share options:*

Use the Share button to share the link to the article, donate it, or add it to your wishlist.

### 3. **Wishlist**:

Add items to your wishlist for future reference.

**Buy & Download:**

### 1. Buy:

To buy an item, tap the price. If it's free, tap "Get". If you've already purchased the item, you'll see a Download button instead of the price.

### 2. Authentication:

Authenticate your Apple ID using Face ID, Touch ID, or your password to complete the purchase.

### 3. Download Progress:

To check your download progress, tap "More" then "Download."

**Redeem gift card**

**Redeem or send a gift card:**

Tap "Music," scroll down, then tap "Redeem" or "Send gift" to redeem or send App Store and iTunes gift cards.

# Journal

To get started with Journal on your iPhone, follow these steps:

## Set up Journal:

1. After updating to iOS 17. 2, open the Journal app.

2. Follow the onscreen instructions to enable and customize logging suggestions.

## Create a journal entry:

1. Press the Compose button in the Journal application.

2. Select "New Items" or choose from personalized recommendations based on your recent activities.

3. Start writing your entry and add details like photos, audio, and location.

**Check your entries:**

1. Scroll through your diary to see previous entries.

2. Press the Filter button to view entries of certain types, such as photos or conversations.

**Lock your diary:**

1. Protect your diary with Face ID, Touch ID or your password.

2. Go to Settings > Log > Key Log, then turn on Lock.

## Write a diary:

1. Open the Diary app on your iPhone.

2. Tap Compose and select "New entry" or journaling proposal.

3. Add photos, videos, audio, and more to your entries.

4. Get suggestions for topics to write about based on your activities.

## Use journaling suggestions:

1. Tap Compose and look through the suggested suggestions.

2. Tap "Write about this" to create a new entry with all suggested attachments.

3. Or tap a suggestion to preview attachments and personalize your entry.

**Add details to entry:**

1. When you write an entry, you can change the date, get recent activity suggestions, add photos/videos, record audio, add map locations, and more.

2. Reorganize or delete attachments if necessary.

3. Bookmark to review later.


**Start importing from another application:**

1. When using another app, tap the Share button.

2. Tap "Diary" (if not visible, add it to sharing options).

3. Enter your thoughts and press Save.


*By following these steps, you can effectively use the Diary app on your iPhone to record your thoughts,*

*memories, and experiences.*

# Magnifier

To use the Magnifier app on iPhone to zoom in and examine objects around you, follow these steps:

## Turn on Magnifier:

1. Open the Magnifier app by tapping its icon on the d screen of your iPhone or by accessing it through Siri.

2. You can also open Control Center and tap the Magnifier button.

## Orthopedics:

1. In the Magnifier app, adjust the zoom level by dragging the slider left or right.

2. Use controls such as brightness, contrast, color filters, torch, and focus lock to enhance images.

**Freeze Image:**

1. Press the Freeze Image button to take and review the image.

2. You can freeze multiple images and view them individually.

**Using detection mode (on supported models):**

1. Press the Detection Mode button to access features such as person detection, door detection, room depiction, text detection, pointing detection and voice.

2. Customize person detection settings, such as units, sound distance, and feedback.

**Read text and labels aloud:**

1. In discovery mode, use text detection to have your iPhone read all displayed text aloud.

2. Use point and talk to identify and have iPhone read aloud interactive labels around you.

**Configure Shortcuts:**

Customize Accessibility Shortcuts to quickly access Discovery Mode through a variety of methods, like triple-tapping, tapping the back of iPhone, or using VoiceOver gestures.

*By following these steps, you can effectively use the Magnifier app on iPhone to magnify objects, detect people and text, and read text aloud.*

# Mail

To manage email accounts on your iPhone, including adding, removing, and customizing them, follow these steps:

## Add an email account:

1. Go to Settings > Mail.
2. Tap Account, then tap Add account.
3. Select the email service you want to use (example: iCloud, Microsoft Exchange) and enter your email account information.

- If your email service is not listed, tap More, then Add Email Account and enter your email account information.

## Temporarily stop using email account:

1.  Go to Settings > Mail > Accounts.

2.  Tap the email account you want to disable.

3.  For an iCloud email account, tap iCloud > iCloud Mail > turn off Use on This iPhone.

4.  For other email accounts, just turn off Mail.


## Delete email account:

1.  Go to Settings > Mail > Accounts.

2.  Tap the email account you want to delete.

3. Tap Sign out or Delete account.

- **Note:** This does not cancel the email account; it will delete it from your iPhone.

*Note: Some courier services may override your selection. For example, iCloud typically doesn't retain deleted emails for more than 30 days, even if you select "Never. "*

**Add Mail app to home screen:**

1. If the Mail app is missing, go to App Library by swiping left on your Home screen.

2. Enter "Mail" in the search box.

3. Touch and hold the Mail app icon, then tap Add to Home Screen.

## Set up a custom email domain with iCloud Mail:

1. Go to Settings > [Your Name] > iCloud > iCloud Mail and make sure "Use on This iPhone" is turned on.

2. Tap Custom Email Domain and choose to buy a domain or use a domain you own.

3. Follow the on-screen instructions to complete setup.

*- Note:* You need a primary iCloud Mail address before adding a custom email domain.

## Delete a custom email domain:

1. Go to Settings > [Your Name] > iCloud > iCloud Mail.
2. Tap Custom Email Domain, then tap Edit next to Your Domain.
3. Press the Delete button, then confirm by pressing Delete.

## Allow all messages to your domain:

1. Go to Settings > [Your Name] > iCloud > iCloud Mail.

2. Tap Custom Email Domain and select your domain.

3. Enable Allow all incoming messages to receive all messages sent to your domain.

*By following these steps, you can easily manage your email account on iPhone, including adding a custom email domain and configuring advanced settings.*

## Maps

To view maps on your iPhone and use various features of the Maps app, follow these steps:

1. **Allow Maps to use your exact location:**

   - Make sure your iPhone is connected to the Internet and location services are turned on.

   - If Maps asks you to turn on location services or precise location, follow the onscreen instructions.

2. **See your current location:**

- Open the Maps app.

- Press the "Turn off tracking"
  button to see your current location
  on the map. You can switch
  between different tracking modes
  to display your heading or to keep
  up with north.

## 3. Choose the right map:

- Press the button in the top right
  corner of the map to select
  different map types, such as
  explore, driving, transit, or
  satellite view.

## 4. View 3D maps:

- On 2D maps, you can switch to 3D view by swiping up with two fingers or tapping the "3D" option at the top right.

- In supported areas, you can also tap "3D" in the top right to see an enhanced 3D map.

- Adjust the angle by sliding two fingers up or down.

- To return to the 2D map, tap "2D" in the top right.

## 5. Move, zoom or rotate the map:

- Drag the map to move.

- Pinch open or close to zoom in or out.

- Touch and hold the card with two fingers to rotate it.

- Press the compass button to display north at the top of the screen after rotating the map.

## 6. Report an issue with Maps:

- If you notice missing or incorrect information on a map, you can report them by opening the Maps app, touching and holding the map, and selecting "Report errors". or by clicking on your

photo. or your initials, by selecting
"Report," then tap "Report new
issue."

*These steps will help you effectively use the Maps app on iPhone to view maps, find locations, and report any problems you encounter.*

# Measure

To measure size with your iPhone using the Measure app, follow these steps:

1. **Open the Measure app:**

   - Locate and open the Measure app on your iPhone.

2. **Start a measurement:**

   - Position your iPhone so that the object you want to measure is in the camera viewfinder.

   - Slowly scan nearby objects with your iPhone's camera.

## 3. Automatically measure rectangle:

- If iPhone detects the edges of a rectangular object, a white box automatically frames the object.

- Tap the white box or "More" button to see the size of the item.

- You can also take a photo of your measurements by pressing the "Take photo" button.

## 4. Manual measurement:

- Align the point in the center of the screen with the measurement starting point.

- Press the "Add" button to mark the
  starting point.
- Slowly move your iPhone to the
  end of the measurement.
- Press the "Add" button again to
  view the measured length.
- You can also take a photo of your
  measurements by pressing the
  "Take photo" button.

5. **Using edge guides (supported
   models):**
   - Position the point in the center of
     the screen along the right edge of
     the object until the guide appears.

- Press the "Add" button to mark the starting point.

- Move slowly along the guide to the end of the measurement.

- Press the "Add" button again to view the measured length.

- You can also take a photo of your measurements by pressing the "Take Photo" button.

## 6. Use ruler view (supported models):

- After measuring the distance between two points, move your iPhone closer to the measurement line until it turns into a ruler, showing the units The length gradually increases.

- You can then take a photo of your measurements by pressing the "Take Photo" button.

7. Measure a person's height (supported models):

- Position your iPhone so that the person you want to measure appears on the screen from head to toe.
- After a while, a straight line will appear on the top of the person's

head (or hair or hat), with a height measurement displayed just below that line.

- You can take a photo of the measurement by pressing the "Take photo" button.

- To save a photo, tap the screenshot in the lower left corner, tap "Done," then select "Save to Photo" or "Save to File. "

*With these steps, you can effectively use the Measure app on iPhone to measure the size of objects and even a person's height.*

# Message

To set up Messages on iPhone, follow
these steps:

1. **Turn on iMessage:**

   - Go to Settings > Messages.

   - Toggle the switch next to
     "iMessage" to turn it on.

2. **Select phone number and email
   address for iMessage:**

   - In Settings > Messages, go to
     "Send and receive. "

   - Choose the phone number and
     email address you want to use with

iMessage by selecting them from

the available options.

## 3. Access messages on all your Apple devices:

Turn on Messages in iCloud:

- Go to Settings > [your name] > iCloud.

- Tap "Messages" to turn it on.

- Confirm Messages are turned on.

## 4. Select another device for SMS/MMS messaging:

- In Settings > Messages, tap "Forward text messages".

- Turn on the device you want to connect to transfer SMS/MMS messages.

## 5. Share your name and photo:

- Open the Messages app on your iPhone.

- Tap the "Edit" button or "Add" button in the chat list.

- Tap "Set up name and photo" and turn on "Share name and photo".

- Customize your photo, name, and who can see your name and photo.

- Click "Save".

## 6. About iMessage on iPhone:

- iMessage is a secure messaging service for sending and receiving messages on Apple devices.

- Messages sent using iMessage appear in blue bubbles.

- iMessages can be sent over Wi-Fi or cellular service.

- Messages sent using iMessage are end-to-end encrypted.

- Report spam or unwanted messages to Apple when using iMessage.

### 7. Send and reply to messages on iPhone:

- Open the Messages app on your iPhone.

Send a message:

- Tap the compose button (pencil icon) at the top of the screen.
- Enter the recipient's phone number, contact name, or Apple ID.
- Enter your message and press the send button.

Reply to message:

- Tap the conversation you want to reply to in the message list.

- Tap the text field, enter your message and hit the send button.


## 8. Take and edit a photo or video in Messages on iPhone:

- Open the Messages app on your iPhone.

- Press the dial button or open an existing chat.

- Tap the Apps button, then tap Camera to take a new photo or video.

- You can also tap Photos to select an existing photo or video.

- Use available editing tools to edit photos or videos.

- Tap "Send" to share a photo or video in the chat.

## 9. Share content in Messages on iPhone:

- Open the Messages app on your iPhone.

- Start a new message or open a conversation.

- Tap the Compose button.

- Enter recipient information or select from contacts.

- Copy and paste content, tap the apps button to access photos, or share content directly from other apps.

## 10. Share your location in Messages on iPhone:

- Open the Messages app on your iPhone.

- Start a new message or open a conversation.

- Tap the Apps button and then tap Location to share your current location or request someone else's

location.

## 11. Recover Deleted Messages on iPhone:

- Open the Messages app on your iPhone.

- Tap Edit in the conversation list.

- Tap Show Recently Deleted or Recently Deleted.

- Select the messages you want to restore and tap Restore.

*Following these steps will help you set up and use Messages on your iPhone efficiently.*

# News

The News app on iPhone provides a comprehensive way to stay informed about the latest news and topics that interest you. Here's how to get started with News on your iPhone:

1. **Go to the News app:**

   - Find the News app on your iPhone's Home screen. If you can't find it, you can search using the Spotlight search function.

2. **Personalize your News Feed:**

   - Tap "Next" at the bottom of the screen.

- In the "Suggested by Siri" section, tap the "Follow" button next to the channels and topics you want to follow.

- To set a favorite channel or topic, tap "Edit", then tap the "Add favorite channel" button next to the channel or topic.

## 3. Receive notification:

- Click "Next. "

- Swipe down from the bottom of the screen and tap "Notifications & email" in Manage.

- Turn on notifications for your
  favorite channels.

## 4. Receive the Apple News newsletter:

- Tap " Next."
- Swipe down to the bottom of the
  screen, then tap "Notifications &
  Email."
- Turn on Apple News newsletter or
  tap 'Subscribe to newsletter' if this
  is your first time.

## 5. Restrict stories in news feed today:

- Go to Settings > News.

- Turn on "Limit today's news"

  Stories. "

## 6. Read Stories:

- Tap a story in the Today feed to

  read it.

- Swipe left or right to read the next

  or previous story.

- Tap the channel name at the top of

  the story to see the channel feed.

## 7. Follow, unfollow, block and unblock channels and topics:

- Long press on a story to access
  options.

- Tap the channel name to go to the
  channel feed.

- At the top of the feed, tap to follow,
  unfollow, block, or unblock
  channels and topics.

**8. Manage favorites:**

- Tap "Next", then tap "Edit".

- Add or remove channels and topics
  from your favorites.

- Reorder your favorites as you like.

## 9. Stop suggesting specific channels and topic groups:

- Tap "Today".

- Tap the More button in a channel or topic group, then tap "Stop Suggesting."


## 10. Let News know your preferences:

- Press "Today".

- Tap the More button below the title, then tap "Suggest more" or "Suggest less. "

*Once you set up and customize your News app, you'll start receiving updates and stories based on your interests and preferences. You can always adjust your settings and preferences to fine-tune the News experience on your iPhone.*

# Notes

To start using Notes on iPhone, follow these steps:

## Write a quick note:

1. *Open any app:* You can take a quick note from any app any application or screen.

2. *Tap the Share button:* Find the Share button in the app or screen you're using.

3. *Select "Quick new note":* This option allows you to quickly create a new note.

4. **Add content:** You can add text, images, links, and more to your quick notes.

## Add sketches and more:

1. **Open Note:** Create a new note or open an existing note.

2. **Tap the Inking Tools button:** This button allows you to access drawing and markup tools.

3. **Start drawing or writing:** Use your finger to draw or write directly on the note.

4. **_Explore markup tools:_**

Experiment with different tools,

colors, and rulers to draw accurately.

## Scan a document:

1. **_Open a note:_** Create a new note or

   open an existing note where you want

   to save the scanned document.

2. **_Press camera button:_** In notes,

   press the camera button.

3. **_Select "Scan Documents":_** Select

   this option to enable the document

   scanner.

4. ***Position your iPhone:*** Position your iPhone so that the document page appears on the screen.

5. ***Scan Document:*** Your iPhone automatically scans the page. Once scanned, you can save it to notes and even add your signature.

## Organize with tags and smart folders:

1. ***Label your notes:*** Use "#" followed by the tag name to categorize and organize your notes.

2. ***Add multiple tags:*** You can add multiple tags to a note to improve organization.

3. ***Search & Filter:*** Easily search and filter your notes in folders using tags.

## Create and format notes:

1. ***Create a new note:*** Open the Notes app on your iPhone and tap the "New Note" button.

2. **Enter your text:** Enter your note content. The first line automatically becomes the note's title.

3. **Format text:** Select the text you want to format and press the "Format" button to select the style.

## Add a checklist:

1. **Open a note:** In the note, press the "Checklist" button.

2. **Add item:** Enter text and press Return to add item to the checklist.

3. **Manage checklists:** You can mark items as complete, reorder items, and manage checklists using menu options.

## Add or edit a table:

1. *Open a note:* Click the "Add table" button in the note.

2. *Enter text:* Tap a cell to enter text. You can move to the next cell by pressing next.

3. *Format Table:* Format rows or columns, add or delete rows or columns, and move rows or columns as needed.

**Draw or write in Notes:**

1. *Open the Notes app:* Launch the Notes app on your iPhone.

2. *Access inking tools:* Tap the "Inking tools" button in the note.

3. ***Draw or write:*** Use your finger to draw or write directly on the note.

4. ***Explore markup tools:*** Experiment with different colors and tools to improve your drawings or handwritten notes.

**Lock your notes:**

1. ***Set a password:*** Go to Settings > Notes > Password to set a password to lock your notes.

2. ***Choose a lock method:*** You can use your device passcode or a custom password to lock your notes.

3. **Lock individual notes:** Open a note, tap the Note Actions button, then tap "Lock" to secure the note.

**Customize note settings:**

1. **Go to Settings:** Go to Settings > Notes to customize your Notes app settings.

2. **Set default account:** Choose a default account for new notes, set a password, and adjust other options to your needs.

*By following these steps, you can effectively use the Notes app on iPhone to record, organize, and secure your*

*thoughts and information.*

# Phone

To make a call on iPhone, you can follow these steps:

## Dial:

1. ***Open the Phone app:*** Find and open the Phone app on your iPhone.

2. ***Tap "Keypad":*** This will display the dial pad interface.

3. ***Enter number:*** Using the keypad, enter the phone number you want to call.

   - If you write incorrectly, press the "Delete" button to correct it.

- You can also paste the number you copied by tapping the phone number field and selecting "Paste".

4. **Make a call:** Press the green "Call" button to start the call.

5. **End Call:** After your call ends, you can end it by pressing the red "End Call" button.

## Call your favorite person:

1. **Tap "Favorites":** In the Phone app, tap the "Favorites" tab.

2. **Select contact:** Select the contact from your favorites list that you want to call.

3. ***Start a call:*** Tap the contact's phone number to start the call.

## Call back or forward recent calls:

1. ***Tap "Recent":*** Go to the "Recent" tab in the Phone app.
2. ***Select Call:*** Select the number from the recent calls list that you want to call back or forward.
3. ***Start a call:*** Tap the contact's phone number to start the call.

– You can press the "More Info" button to get more information about the call or the caller.

**Call someone from your contact list:**

1. **Open Contacts:** Launch the Contacts app on your iPhone.

2. **Select Contact:** Tap the contact you want to call.

3. **Select a number:** If the contact has multiple phone numbers, select the number you want to call.

4. **Start call:** Tap the phone number to start the call.

**Adjust call settings:**

1. **Go to Phone Settings:** Go to Settings > Phone on your iPhone.

2. *Customize settings:* In phone
settings, you can adjust various call
settings such as displaying caller ID,
enabling Dialing Assist for
international calls, etc.

**Use Wi-Fi Calling:**

1. *Turn on Wi-Fi Calling:* Go to
Settings > Cellular > Wi-Fi Calling.

2. *Enable Wi-Fi calling:* Toggle the
switch to turn on Wi-Fi calling on
your iPhone.

3. *Set up Wi-Fi calling:* Enter or
confirm your address for emergency
services if prompted.

**Avoid unwanted calls:**

1. *Call identification:* Go to Settings > Phone > Call blocking & Call identification to enable call identification features such as Business Connect ID, 'Call ID from operator and call identification application.

2. *Block contacts:* You can block unwanted callers by tapping a contact in your Recent, Favorites, or Voicemail list, selecting "More Info," scrolling down, and tapping "Block this caller".

3. **Send unknown and unwanted callers to voicemail:** In Settings > Phone, you can turn on features like "Silence unknown callers" and "Silence unwanted callers" to send unknown callers and unwanted messages directly to voicemail.

*By following these steps, you can effectively make calls, manage contacts, and customize call settings on your iPhone.*

# Photos

To view photos and videos in the Photos app on iPhone, follow these steps:

**Organize photos and videos:**

1. *Gallery:* Tap the "Gallery" button to browse photos and videos have been sorted. by day, month, year or view all photos.

2. *For you:* Explore memories, shared photos, and featured photos in a personalized feed.

3. *Albums:* See albums you've created or shared, with your photos automatically sorted by categories like

People & Animals, Places, and Media
Type.

4. *Search:* Use the search box to search
for photos by date, location, caption,
or object in the photo.

**Browse photos:**

1. *Browse your gallery:* Tap
"Gallery" and choose a view like Year,
Month, Day or All Photos.

2. *View individual photos:* Click on
the photo to view full screen.
  - Double tap or pinch to zoom
    in/out.

- Press the Favorite button to add
  photos to your Favorites album.

- For Live Photos, tap and hold to
  play the animation.

3. ***View photo information:*** Tap the
   Info button or swipe up to see details
   like who's tagged, caption, location,
   camera metadata, and more.

## Play videos and slideshows:

1. ***Play video:*** Tap the video to play.
   Use the player controls to pause,
   unmute, add to favorites, share, or
   delete.

2. ***Create a slideshow:*** Select photos, tap Add, then tap Slideshow. Adjust settings like theme and music.

**Delete and edit photos:**

1. ***Delete or hide a photo:*** Tap the photo, then delete or hide it using the More button.

2. ***Recover deleted photos:*** Go to the recently deleted album in Album to restore or permanently delete photos.

3. ***Edit a photo:*** Tap Edit to adjust lighting, color, crop, rotate, apply filters, write or draw, and more. Undo and redo changes if necessary.

**iCloud Photos:**

1. ***Turn on iCloud Photos:*** In Settings > [your name] > iCloud > Photos, turn on iCloud Photos to sync your photos and videos across devices.

2. ***Save Space:*** Optimize iPhone storage to keep full-resolution photos in iCloud and space-saving versions on your iPhone.

3. ***Get more storage:*** Upgrade to iCloud+ to get more storage and features when you need it.

*By following these steps, you can efficiently browse, view, organize, and edit your photos and videos using the Photos app on iPhone.*

# Podcast

To find, listen to, and manage podcasts on your iPhone using the Podcasts app, follow these steps:

## Search for podcasts

1. **Search for podcasts:**

   - Open the Podcasts app and tap "Search" at the bottom right.

   - Enter a title, person or topic you are interested in and press "Search" on the keyboard.

2. **Discover new shows:**

   - Tap "Browse" at the bottom to explore new and trending shows,

as well as Apple's editorial
collections.

- You can also press "Search" to see
top charts and browse by category.

## 3. Add a show by URL:

- Go to the Library tab, press the
Add button, then press "Follow a
show by URL" and enter the
podcast's RSS URL.

## Personalized recommendations

## 1. Up Next Suggestions:

- The "Up Next" section displays episode suggestions based on your listening history.
- Tap "Home" at the bottom of the screen to see a list of suggestions.
- Tap the More button below an episode to perform actions such as downloading, saving, or removing the episode from Up Next.

## 2. Turn off personalized recommendations:

- If you want to turn off personalized recommendations, go to Home, tap your profile picture, then your name, and turn off

"Suggestions personalized".

## Currently sharing podcasts

## Shared with friends:

- When a friend shares a show with you in Messages, you can find the show in the Podcasts app.

- Tap "Home" at the bottom, then scroll down to "Shared with you."

## Browse episodes

## In a specific podcast:

- Tap a show to see its info page.

- Scroll to see recent episodes or tap "See All" if available.

## Listen to Podcast

### 1. Play Podcast:

- Press the play button below the episode title to start playing.
- You can also tap an episode in the Up Next section.

### 2. Choose what to read next:

- Add episodes to "Play Next" by tapping the episode's Add button and selecting "Add to queue. "

- Manage the queue by tapping the player at the bottom, then tap the "Play Next" button.

## 3. Set a sleep timer:

- Open the Playback in progress screen, tap Sleep Timer button and select

## 4. View episode transcripts:

- If available, press the Show Transcript button to read the full transcript.

## 5. Use Playback Controls:

- Use controls such as Play, Pause, Playback Speed, Skip, AirPlay, etc., on the Now Playing screen.

## Follow a podcast

## 1. Follow a podcast:

- Tap a show then tap "Follow" in the top right.
- You can also press the More button and select "Follow the program".

## 2. Unfollow Podcast:

- Tap a show you follow, tap the
  More button, then select "Unfollow
  Show".

**New episode notifications**

**Turn on notifications**

- Tap "Home", then tap your profile
  picture and go to notifications to
  turn it on or off.

# Reminders

To add or remove accounts in the
Reminders app on iPhone and create and
manage lists in the app, follow these
steps:

## Add or remove accounts

1. **Add account:**

   - Go to Settings > Reminders >
     Accounts > Add account.

   - Select your account provider from
     the list or tap "Other" if it is not
     listed.

   - Enter your account information
     and enable reminders for this
     account.

## 2. Delete account:

- Temporarily stop using account:

- Go to Settings > Reminders > Account.

- Tap the account, then turn off the reminder.

- To show reminders for this account again on your iPhone, turn on Reminders.

- Delete account:

- Go to Settings > Reminders > Account.

- Tap the account you want to delete.

- Tap "Sign out" (for iCloud accounts) or "Delete account" (for other accounts).

## Create and manage lists

## 1. Create a new grocery list:

- Open the Reminders app on iPhone.

- Tap "Add List," then select an account.

- Enter a name for the list, tap "List type," then select "Grocery."

- You can optionally choose the color and symbol for the list.

## 2. Add items to your grocery list:

- In your grocery list, tap "Items new", then enter an item description.

- Tap "Add Note" to add additional information.

- Tap "Edit Details" to further personalize the item.


## 3. Show list in columns:

- In your shopping list, tap the More button, then tap "Show as columns."

- Recategorize items by dragging them into different columns.

## 4. Create custom items:

- In your grocery list, tap the Add button, then tap "Manage items. "

- Tap "New Section", then enter a name.

- Rename or reorder sections as needed.

## 5. Edit and manage sections:

- Mark sections are complete by tapping the empty circle next to them.

- Edit multiple items at once by selecting them and using the buttons at the bottom.

- Organize related items using sections.

- Create subtasks by swiping right on an item or dragging it onto another item.

- Sort and reorder items manually or by due date, creation date, priority, or title.

- Delete an item by dragging it to the left and pressing "Delete".

## Using Smart List

1. **Automatically sort items:**

   - Show default smart lists like
     Today, Scheduled, Bookmarked,
     Done, Assigned to me, and Siri
     Suggestions.

   - To show, hide, or rearrange the
     default smart list, tap the More
     button, then tap "Edit List."

2. **Create a custom smart list:**

   - Tap "Add List," enter a name,
     choose a color and icon, then tap
     "Create Smart List."

- Choose filters like tags, dates, locations, etc. to automatically include relevant entries.

## 3. Add item to smart list:

- Select the list, tap "New reminder" then enter text.
- The item inherits smart list properties and is saved in your default list.

# Safari

To browse the web using Safari on your iPhone, follow these steps:

1. **Open Safari:**

   - Locate the Safari app icon on your iPhone's Home screen and tap it to Launch the Safari browser.

2. **Enter a website URL or search term:**

   - Tap the address bar at the top of the Safari window.

   - Enter the URL of the website you want to visit, or enter a search term to search the web.

### 3. Browse websites:

- After you enter a URL or search term, Safari loads the website.

- You can scroll up and down to view web page content.

### 4. Navigate back and forth:

- To return to a previously visited web page, tap the back arrow located in the upper left corner.

- To move to the next website (if available), press the forward arrow button next to the back arrow.

## 5. Refresh Page:

- To refresh the current web page and load the latest content, you can scroll down until the wheel appears and then release to refresh.

## 6. Share link:

- To share a link to the current web page, tap the share button at the bottom of the Safari window.

- You can then choose from different options to share the link via text, email, social networks, etc.

## 7. Preview of site links:

- Press and hold a link in a web page to see a preview of the linked page without fully opening it.

- Tap the preview to open the link or choose other options like open in new tab, add to reading list or copy link.

## 8. Web page translation:

- If you come across a website in a foreign language, Safari may offer to translate the page for you if a translation is available.

- Tap the Page Setup button, then tap the Translate button if prompted.

## 9. Customize start page:

- You can customize Safari's start page with your favorite websites, frequently visited websites, shared links, and more.
- Press the Tab button, then press the New Tab button to go to the start page. Scroll down and tap Edit to customize.

**10. Change text size and display controls:**

- Adjust text size and display settings for your website by tapping the Page Settings button and selecting options like increase/decrease text size or hide search box.

**11. Browsing in private mode:**

- Safari offers a private browsing mode that does not save your browsing history or cookies.
- Tap the Tab button, swipe right on the tab bar until you see Incognito,

then tap to go into Incognito
mode.

12.  **Tab management:**

-   You can open multiple tabs in
    Safari to browse multiple websites
    at the same time.
-   Tap the Tab button to see all open
    tabs, swipe left or right to close
    tabs, or tap the New Tab button to
    open a new tab.

13.  **Show Privacy Report:**

-   Safari offers a privacy reporting
    feature that shows you which

trackers have been blocked while browsing the web.

- Tap the Site Settings button, then tap Privacy Report to view the report.

14. **Adjust privacy and security settings:**

- Customize Safari privacy and security settings by going to Settings > Safari and toggling options like Prevent Cross-Site Tracking , Hide IP address, Fraudulent website warning, etc.

## 15. Use passcode:

- If sites support it, you can use Face ID or Touch ID to sign in securely without entering a password.

- Safari may prompt you to use Face ID or Touch ID for supported websites.

*By following these steps, you can browse the web effectively using Safari on iPhone.*

# Shortcuts

To automate tasks on your iPhone using the Shortcuts app, follow these steps:

1. **Open the Shortcuts app:**

   - Locate the Shortcuts app on your Home screen of iPhone and tap on that app to open it.

2. **Browse or create shortcuts:**

   - ***Browse available shortcuts:*** Tap the "Library" tab at the bottom to explore predefined shortcuts created by Apple and created by other users. You can search for specific types of

shortcuts or browse categories.

-   ***Create your own shortcut:*** If

    you want to create your own

    custom shortcut, tap the "My

    Shortcuts" tab, then tap the "+"

    button to start creating a shortcut

    from scratch.


3. **Select or create a shortcut:**

-   If you find a predefined shortcut in

    the library, tap it to view details

    and customize if needed. Then tap

    "Add Shortcut" to add it to your

    collection.

- If you create your own shortcuts, use available actions and features to create your custom workflow. You can add actions from various apps, set variables, create conditions, and more.

## 4. Customize shortcut settings:

- After adding a shortcut, you can customize its settings by tapping it in the "My Shortcuts" tab.
- You can change the shortcut's name, add a custom icon, assign a Siri Phrase to activate the shortcut with a voice command, and more.

5. **Run Shortcut**:

   - To run a shortcut, simply tap it in the Shortcuts app. It will automatically perform the sequence of actions you configured.

   - You can also run shortcuts by asking Siri. Just say the Siri phrase you assigned to the shortcut and Siri will do it for you.

# Stocks

To check stocks on your iPhone using the Stocks app, follow these steps:

1. **Open the Stocks app:**

   - Locate the Stocks app on your iPhone home screen and tap the app to open it.

2. **Show My Symbols Watchlist:**

   - When you first open the Stocks app, you will see My Symbols Watchlist, which displays a list of symbols securities and their performance.

- Tap a stock icon in the watchlist to see more details about that stock.

## 3. Search for a specific stock:

- If you want to search for a specific stock, enter the stock code, company name, fund name or index in the search box at the top of the screen.

- Tap the icon in the search results to see details.

## 4. View charts, details and news:

- After selecting a stock, you can view interactive charts,

performance details and related news.

- You can tap options from the time range selections at the top of the chart to see performance over time.

- Touch and hold the chart to view values for a specific date or time.

- Drag data below the chart to see additional details such as 52-week high and low, beta, EPS, and average trading volume.

- Swipe up to see more news related to the selected title.

**5.** **Manage symbols in the My Symbols watchlist:**

To make changes to the My Symbols watchlist, you can add, remove or reorder symbols:

- *Add symbol:* In the search field, enter a symbol. or company name, tap the Add button in the search results, then tap Done.

- *Delete icon:* Swipe left on the icon in your watchlist and tap the delete option.

- *Rearrange Icons:* Touch and hold an icon in your watchlist, then drag it to a new location.

## 6. Create and manage multiple watchlists:

- You can create your own watchlist to organize stocks into categories.

- Tap "My icons", then tap "New watchlist" to create a new watchlist. Name the watchlist and press Save.

- To switch between watchlists, tap "My icon" or the name of the current watchlist and select the list you want to view.

- You can add symbols to the watchlist, remove symbols from the watchlist, sort symbols, change the displayed value, delete the

watchlist, reorder the list Track

and view your watchlist on all your

devices using iCloud.


 *By following these steps, you can*

*effectively use the Stocks app on iPhone*

*to track market activity and monitor the*

*performance of the stocks you follow.*

# Tips

To get tips on your iPhone and take full advantage of its features, follow these steps:

1. **Open the Tips app:**

   - Locate the Tips app on your Home screen of iPhone and tap on that app to open it.

2. **Explore Tip Collections:**

   - In the Tips app, you'll find collections of tips that cover various aspects of using iPhone effectively.

- Tap the collection you're interested in to see tips within it.

## 3. View and learn tips:

- Once you've selected a collection, tap a specific tip to learn more.
- Tips cover a variety of topics, from basic to advanced iPhone features.

## 4. Get notified about new tips:

If you want to be notified when there are new tips, you can turn on notifications for the Tips app:

- Go to Settings > Notifications.

- Tap "Tips" under Notification style, then turn on Allow notifications.
- Customize notification settings according to your preferences.

## 5. Save Useful Tips:

If you come across a tip that you find particularly useful and want to review later, you can save it:

- Just press the Save button Link to that tip.
- You can access your saved tips later by going to the "Saved Tips" collection in the Tips app.

- To remove a tip from your saved

  tip collection, tap the "Delete

  Saved Tip" button.

# Translations

To translate text, voice, and even conversations on your iPhone, you can use the Translate app. Here's how:

**Translate text or voice:**

1. Open the Translate app on your iPhone.
2. Select the language you want to translate into.
3. To swap languages, tap the Swap languages button.
4. Tap one of the following options:
   - *Translate text:* Tap "Enter text," type or paste the text, then tap Next or Done.

- Translate your voice: Press the Listen button and speak the sentence.

5. The translation will appear. You can:

    - Press the Play button to listen to the audio translation.

    - Press the Enter button in full screen mode to show the translation to others.

    - Click the Favorites button to save the translation.

    - Click the Copy button to copy the translation.

**Conversation translation:**

1. Tap the Conversations tab.

2. Select how you want to enter text (type or voice).

3. Start chatting. Every message will be translated.

4. You can press the Play button to listen to the translation.

**Review of multiple meaning words:**

1. Translate a word or phrase.

2. If a word has multiple meanings, tap the word to select the desired meaning.

3. You can also choose a grammatical gender translation if available.

417

## Download languages for offline use:

1. Go to Settings > Translate.

2. Tap Downloaded Language.

3. Tap the Download button next to the language you want to download.

## Translate text in apps:

1. Select text in apps like Safari, Messages, or Mail.

2. Tap Translate.

3. Select the language you want to translate into.

4. Below Translations, you can replace the original text, copy the translation, add to favorites, or open in the Translate app.

**Translate text in photos:**

1. In the Photos app, view photos with text.

2. Press the Detect Text button.

3. Touch and hold the text you want to translate, then tap Translate.

4. You can also use the Camera app to translate text in real time or translate text from photos in the Translate app.

**Share and save translation:**

1. After translating, click the Share button.

2. Select the sharing option or tap Save Image to save the translation as an image.

*By following these steps, you can effectively translate text, voice, and conversations on iPhone using the Translate app.*

# Apple TV

To subscribe to Apple TV+, MLS Season Pass, or Apple TV on your iPhone, follow these steps:

### Subscribe to Apple TV+:

1. Open the Apple TV app on your iPhone.
2. Tap "Apple TV+".
3. Click the register button.
4. Check your free trial (if eligible) and subscription information.
5. Follow the on-screen instructions to complete registration.

### Sign up for MLS Season Pass:

1. Tap "Search" in the Apple TV app.

2. Search for "MLS Season Pass".

3. Click the register button.

4. Review the subscription details and select the subscription option.

5. Follow the on-screen instructions to complete registration.

## Subscribe to Apple TV channels and apps:

1. Tap "Store" in the Apple TV app.

2. Scroll down to "Add channels and apps".

3. Swipe left to browse, then tap an item.

4. Click the register button.

5. Check out the free trial (if eligible) and subscription details.

6. Follow the on-screen instructions to complete registration.

**Change or cancel your subscription:**

1. Tap "Home" in the Apple TV app.

2. Tap your photo or initials at the top right.

3. Click "Manage subscription".

4. Follow the on-screen instructions to change or cancel your subscription.

## Share subscription with family members:

Apple TV+, MLS Season Pass, and Apple TV Channel subscriptions can be shared with up to five other family members using the feature family sharing.

## Add your TV provider:

1. Go to Settings > TV Provider on your iPhone.
2. Select your TV provider and sign in with your credentials.

## Watch sports on the Apple TV app:

1. Open the Apple TV app on your iPhone.

2. Press "Home" and move to the "Sports" line.

3. Browse live and upcoming matches or tap "Live Sports" to filter by sport.

4. Click on the live match to watch.

**Change Apple TV app settings:**

1. Go to Settings > TV on your iPhone.

2. Adjust streaming and download options, including mobile data usage and download quality.

3. Change how your watch history is used for personalized recommendations.

4. Customize your device preferences, like showing or hiding live sports scores.

# Voice Memos

To record to Voice Memos on iPhone, follow these steps:

**Basic recording:**

1. Open the Voice Memos app on your iPhone.
2. Press the Record button (red circle) to start recording.
3. Adjust the recording level by moving the microphone closer or farther from the sound source.
4. When finished recording, press the Stop button (red square) to finish.
5. Your recording will be saved with the default name "New Recording" or

your location name if location services are enabled. You can tap the record to rename it if needed.

## Advanced recording:

1. Follow steps 1 to 3 of the basic recording guide to start recording.

2. Swipe down from the top of the waveform to see more details while recording.

3. Tap the Pause button (two vertical lines) to pause recording, then tap Resume to continue.

4. After recording, press the Play button (triangle) to review your recording.

5. You can drag the waveform left or right to change where playback starts.

6. Click Done to save the recording.

7. Your recording will be saved under the default name "New Record" or your location name. You can rename it by clicking save.

**Mute the startup and shutdown sounds:**

- To mute the startup and shutdown sounds, use the volume down button on iPhone while recording.

**Recording with another app:**

- You can switch to another app while recording to Voice Memos, as long as that app is not playing audio. If audio playback starts in another app, Voice Memos will stop recording.

## Dynamic Island (iPhone 14 Pro and later):

- On compatible iPhones, you can see your recording progress in Dynamic Island at the top of your Home screen and in other apps. You can tap the animation to return to the voice memo. Press and hold the motion to expand it, and you can stop recording without returning to the voice memo.

*By following these steps, you can easily create audio recordings using the Voice Memos app on iPhone.*

# Wallet

To store cards and cards in Wallet on iPhone, follow these steps:

## Add a card to Wallet:

1. Open the Wallet app on your iPhone.

2. Press the "+" button to add a new card.

3. Follow the onscreen instructions to add a debit or credit card, Apple Card, or other supported cards.

4. You can also add cards from supported apps or cards previously used with Apple Pay.

## View card details and settings:

1. Open the Wallet app.

2. Tap the card you want to view or manage.

3. Press the "Add" button (. . .) to view card details and change settings.

4. You can view card number, card details, notification settings, etc.

**Connect account to wallet:**

1. Open the Wallet app.

2. Click on the card you want to connect to.

3. If yes, tap "Get Started" and follow the onscreen instructions to connect your account.

4. With accounts connected, you can view account balances and transaction history in the Wallet.

## Change Apple Pay settings:

1. Go to Settings > Wallet & Apple Pay.

2. Adjust settings like double-click actions, allowing payments on your Mac, and more.

## Track your order in Wallet:

1. Open the Wallet app.

2. Press the "Command" button.

3. Track your order automatically or manually by tapping "Track with Apple Wallet" on the order confirmation screen.

## Organize cards and cards:

1. To set a default payment card, touch and hold a card, then drag it to the front of the stack.

2. To rearrange cards, keys, and tags, touch and hold the item, then drag it to a new location.

3. To hide or archive expired cards, go to Settings > Wallet & Apple Pay, then turn on "Hide expired cards."

4. To view or restore expired cards, scroll to the bottom of the stack in Wallet, tap "Show expired cards," select the card, and tap "View."

5. To permanently delete a card, see the "Remove card or pass from wallet" option.

*By following these steps, you can manage your cards, keys, passes, and orders easily effectively in the Wallet app on iPhone.*

# Weather

To check the weather on iPhone using the Weather app, follow these steps:

## Check local conditions and forecasts:

1. Open the Weather app on your iPhone.

2. By default, the app displays details about your current location. If not, tap the "Edit City" button, then tap "My Location."

3. Swipe up to see weather details such as hourly forecast, 10-day forecast, severe weather alerts, maps, air

quality, news and additional weather details.

## Customize weather units:

1. Open the Weather App on your iPhone.

2. Click the Edit City button.

3. Click the "Add" button, then click "Units".

4. Change the unit of temperature, wind, precipitation, pressure or distance to your preference.

## Send weather forecast:

1. Open the Weather app on your iPhone.

2. Click the "Edit city" button, then click the "Add" button.

3. Tap "Report a problem," select options that accurately describe weather conditions, then tap "Submit."

**Check the weather in other locations:**

1. Open the Weather app on your iPhone.

2. Tap the "Favorites" button in the lower right corner.

3. Enter the city, county, or location name in the search box.

4. Tap a location in the search results to see the forecast.

5. To add a location to your weather list, tap "Add" after selecting the location from the search results.

## Delete and reorder locations in the weather list:

1. Open the Weather app on your iPhone.

2. Click the "Edit city" button to see your weather list.

3. To delete a location, swipe left on it and tap "Delete" or tap the "Add" button, then tap "Edit List. "

4. To reorder positions, touch and hold a position, then move it up or down. You can also tap the "Add" button and then tap "Edit List". "

*By following these steps, you can effectively check the weather in your current location, customize units, report weather issues, and manage weather lists on iPhone using the Weather app.*

# SIRI

## Use Siri on Your iPhone

### Set up Siri:

1. If you haven't set up Siri yet, go to Settings > Siri & Search.

2. Choose how you want to activate Siri: "Hey Siri" or by pressing the side button (on iPhones with Face ID) or the Home button (on iPhones with a Home button).

3. If you select "Hey Siri," follow the instructions to instruct Siri to recognize your voice.

4.  If you choose button activation, turn on "Press side button for Siri" (on iPhones with Face ID) or "Press Home for Siri" (on iPhones with Home button).

## Activate Siri:

### 1. *With your voice:*

-   Say "Hey Siri" or simply "Siri" followed by your question or request.
-   For example, you can say: "Hey Siri, what's the weather today?"" or "Siri, set an alarm for 8 a. m. "

### 2. *By pressing the button:*

- On an iPhone with Face ID, press

  and hold the Side button.

- On an iPhone with a Home button,

  press and hold the Home button.

- With supported EarPods or

  CarPlay, press and hold the

  appropriate button.

- Siri will respond audibly or

  silently, depending on your device

  settings and configuration.

**Make a follow request:**

- After activating Siri, you can make

  a follow request without turning it

  back on.

- For example, you can say: "Hey Siri, how's the weather in San Francisco?" And in Cupertino?
- You can also interrupt Siri while she's speaking to correct or ignore the request.

**Correct if Siri misunderstands you:**

- If Siri misunderstands you, repeat your request another way.
- Press the Listen button to edit your request without reactivating Siri.

- You can also spell out part of your request or edit your request in writing.

**Tap instead of talking to Siri:**

- Go to Settings > Accessibility > Siri and turn on "Tap to Siri".
- Activate Siri, then use the keyboard and text field to type your question or request instead of speaking.

# Find Out What Siri Can Do on iPhone

To use Siri on your iPhone for a variety of tasks and requests, follow these examples:

## Answer questions:

- Activate Siri and ask questions like:

- "What causes Rainbows?"

- "What does a cat look like?"

- "What is the derivative of cosine x?"

- "How do you say thank you in Mandarin?"

## Use Siri with apps:

- When Siri is on, interact with apps using voice commands like:

- "Set up a Meeting with Gordon at 9" to create an event in Calendar.

- "Add artichokes to my grocery list" to add an item to the reminder.

- "Send a message to PoChun saying I love you heart emoji" to send a message using Messages.

- "What is my update?" to get weather updates, news, reminders, calendar events, and more.

## Share information with contacts:

Share multiple screen items with contacts using Siri. For example:

- When viewing a photo, say "Send to Mom" to create a new message with the photo attached.

**Personalize the Siri experience:**

- Customize Siri to better suit your needs and preferences:
- Enable Siri Suggestions for personalized suggestions.
- Talk to Siri about yourself to increase her knowledge.
- Adjust Siri settings to change how and when Siri responds.

# Tell Siri About Yourself on iPhone

To personalize your experience with Siri and enable features like directions home or specific contacts using FaceTiming, follow these steps:

1.  **Tell Siri who you are:**

    - Open the Contacts app on your iPhone and make sure your contact information is filled out.

    - Go to Settings > Siri & Search > My Info.

    - Tap your name in the list to set your contact card as information for Siri.

## 2. Teach Siri to say your name:

- Open the Contacts app and find your contact card.

- Tap "Edit," then scroll down and tap "Add field."

- Select the name pronunciation field and enter the pronunciation of your name.

## 3. Talk to Siri about relationships:

- Activate Siri and say commands like "Hey Siri, Eliza Block is my wife" or "Hey Siri, Ashley Kamin is my mother. "

## 4. Keep Siri settings up to date on all devices:

- Make sure all your Apple devices are signed in with the same Apple ID.
- If you use iCloud, your Siri settings will be synced across
- If you don't want to sync Siri Personalization between devices, you can turn off Siri in iCloud Settings by going to Settings > [Your Name] > iCloud, then turn off Siri.

*Note:* If Location Services is turned on, your device's location at the time of the request will be sent to Apple to improve Siri accuracy. Additionally, Apple may use the IP address of your Internet connection to approximate your location in order to provide relevant responses.

# Change Siri Settings on iPhone

To adjust Siri settings on your iPhone, follow these steps:

### 1. Change Siri response settings:

- Open Settings on your iPhone.

- Scroll down and tap "Siri & Search".

- Customize Siri's response behavior by doing one of the following:

  - To disable "Hey Siri" voice activation, turn off "Listen for 'Hey Siri'. "

  - To prevent Siri from responding to the Side or Home button, turn off

"Press Side button for Siri" (on devices with Face ID) or "Press Home button for Siri" (on devices with Welcome button).

- To limit access to Siri when your iPhone is locked, turn off "Allow Siri when locked."

- To change the language Siri responds to, tap "Language" and select a new language.

## 2. Change Siri voice:

- In Settings > Siri & Search, tap "Siri Voice".

- Choose a diverse or different voice for Siri.

## 3. Adjust Siri response style:

In Settings > Siri & Search, you can customize how Siri responds:

- Tap "Siri Response".
- Choose when Siri provides voice feedback in "Voice feedback".
- Turn on "Always show Siri captions" to see Siri responses on screen.
- Enable "Always show speech" to display your requests on screen.

## 4. Customize Siri settings for phone, FaceTime, and messages:

In Settings > Siri & Search, you can configure Siri settings for phone, FaceTime, and messages:

- Press "Hang up" to activate Siri to hang up and FaceTime.
- Tap "Automatically send messages" to allow Siri to send messages without confirmation.

## 5. Adjust app search settings for Siri:

In Settings > Siri & Search, you can change which apps appear in search:

- Scroll down and select an application.
- Enable or disable its settings as desired.

## 6. Retrain Siri with your voice:

- In Settings > Siri & Search, turn off "Hear 'Hey Siri'".
- Next, turn "Hear "Hey Siri"" back on to retrain Siri with your voice.

*By following these steps, you can customize Siri's behavior, response style, voice, and access on iPhone based on your preferences.*

# IPHONE SAFETY

# FEATURES

## Contact Emergency Services

To use SOS to contact emergency services on your iPhone, follow these steps:

**Quick emergency call (all countries or regions except India):**

1. Press and hold the button and one of the volume buttons simultaneously until the sliders appear and the Emergency SOS countdown ends, then release the buttons.

## OR

2.  Activate emergency SOS by quickly
    pressing the side button five times. Go
    to Settings > Emergency SOS, then
    turn on "5-Tap Call."

## Quick emergency call (India):

1.  Quickly press the side button 3 times
    until the slider appears and the
    emergency SOS countdown timer
    ends.

## OR

2.  If you've turned on the accessibility
    shortcut, press and hold the side

button and volume button at the same time until the slider appears and a countdown timer. The emergency SOS call ends, then release these buttons.

After initiating an emergency call, your iPhone alerts you to emergency contacts by text message (unless canceled). It will also send your current location (if available) and your emergency contacts will receive updates if your location changes within a period of time after entering SOS mode.

**Dial the emergency number when locked:**

1. On the Passcode screen, tap

   Emergency.

2. Dial the emergency number (e.g. 911

   in the US), then press the Call button.

**SMS Emergency services (not**

**available in all countries or**

**regions):**

1. Open the Messages app and enter 911

   or your local emergency number in the

   'To' field.

2. Enter your emergency.

3. Press the send button.

**Change emergency SOS settings:**

1. Go to Settings > Emergency SOS.

2. Adjust settings if necessary:

   - Enable or disable "Call withhold and release" or "Call with 5 taps".

   - Manage your emergency contacts in the Health app under Set up or edit emergency contacts.

*These steps will allow you to quickly and easily contact emergency services and alert your emergency contacts in the event of an emergency. Be sure to check your service provider's emergency call information to understand the limitations of emergency calls over Wi-Fi.*

# Set up and view your Medical ID

To create your Medical ID and allow emergency services and first responders to access it, follow these steps:

## Create your Medical ID:

1. Open the Health app on your iPhone.

2. Tap your photo at the top right, then tap "Medical ID Card."

3. Tap "Get Started" or "Edit," then enter your information. Include details like allergies, health conditions, medications, blood type, and organ donation status.

4. Under "Emergency Contacts," tap "Add Emergency Contact," then add your contact. These contacts will be notified in the event of an emergency.

5. Tap "Done" when you have finished entering your information.

**Access your Medical ID:**

*From the Home screen shortcut (optional):*

- To quickly access your Medical ID from the Home screen, press and hold Health app icon, then select "Medical ID. "

*From the lock screen:*

- Your medical ID information is accessible from the lock screen of iPhone and Apple Watch.

To allow access to the lock screen, follow these steps:

1. Open the Health app on your iPhone.

2. Tap your photo at the top right, then tap "Medical ID Card."

3. Click "Edit", scroll down and turn on "Show when locked" and "Emergency calls. "

**Access your medical ID with emergency services:**

*On iPhone:*

- First responders can view your medical ID from the lock screen by swiping finger (on iPhone with Face ID) or by pressing the Home button (on iPhone with Touch ID), tapping "Emergency" on the passcode screen, then tapping "Medical ID. "

## *On Apple Watch:*

- On Apple Watch, press and hold the side button until the Emergency SOS slider appears. Drag it to the right, then tap "Medical ID" to access your information.

*By setting up a Medical ID and allowing access on the lock screen, you ensure that important medical information is easily accessible in an emergency, emergency services and first responders.*

# Manage Crash Detection

Crash detection is a feature available on iPhone 14 and later models that detects serious car accidents and helps connect users to emergency services and notify contacts their designated emergency.

### How Accident Detection Works:

1. ***Severe Car Accident Detection:*** When your iPhone detects a serious car accident, it will Enable Accident Detection.

2. ***Automatic emergency calls and alerts:*** When a serious problem is detected, your iPhone will display a

warning. It will automatically initiate an emergency phone call after a 20-second countdown unless the user cancels.

3. *Audio message for emergency services:* If the user does not respond, iPhone plays an audio message for emergency services. This notification informs them of the fatal accident and provides the user's latitude and longitude coordinates as well as an approximate search radius.

4. *Does not replace existing emergency calls:* The accident detection feature does not replace any

existing emergency calls made by other means.

5. *Use Emergency SOS Satellite:* In areas without cellular or Wi-Fi connectivity, iPhone will attempt to contact emergency services using Emergency SOS Satellite if Serious error detected.

**Enable or disable collision detection:**

1. *Default setting:* Collision detection is enabled by default.

2. *Turn off automatic alerts and emergency calls:* Users can turn off

Apple's automatic alerts and emergency calls after a serious car accident by going to Settings > SOS emergency, then turn off "Call after a serious accident". However, third-party apps registered for collision detection will still be notified.

**Integration with CarPlay and Apple Watch:**

*CarPlay Integration:* If iPhone with collision detection enabled connected to your vehicle via CarPlay, crash detection features, including emergency dialing, are routed through your iPhone.

**How to use Apple Watch:** If the user is wearing an Apple Watch at the time of the event, emergency services dialing will be initiated by the iPhone, but collision detection features will be routed through the Apple Watch.

**Note:** In general, collision detection is an important safety feature designed to provide quick assistance to users involved in serious auto accidents, thereby increasing the chances of receiving timely emergency assistance.

# Reset Privacy and Security Settings in An Emergency

iPhone Safety Check provides a quick and convenient way to keep your device and personal information safe. It allows you to quickly stop sharing access to your device and personal data with others in an emergency or if you suspect unauthorized access.

**Steps to use Security Check:**

1. *Go to Security Check Settings:*

   Go to Settings > Privacy & Security > Security Check.

2. **Start Emergency Reset:** Tap "Emergency Reset," then tap "Start Emergency Reset" and follow the on-screen instructions.

**Security Checkup Features:**

**- Change Apple ID Passcode and Password:** Security Checkup helps you easily and quickly change your device passcode and Apple ID password, Improve the security of your device and account.

**- Stop sharing your location with Find My:** You can use Safety Check to stop sharing your location with the Find My app, ensuring your location stays private in school emergency or other incidents.

**- *Restrict Messages and FaceTime:*** Security controls let you restrict Messages and FaceTime to the devices you have on hand, preventing unauthorized access to your communication channels.

**- *Review and update shared information:*** Additionally, Safety Check lets you periodically review and update the information you share with people, apps, and devices, make sure your settings match your preferences and security needs.

## Limitations and considerations:

- ***Information not covered:*** It is important to note that Safety Check cannot review or modify certain types of information, e. g. like accounts and passwords, social sharing, and data shared from other devices. .

*Using Safety Check on iPhone, you can proactively manage your device's security and privacy settings, helping to protect your personal information and*

*provide peace of mind.*

# FAMILY SHARING

To set up Family Sharing on your iPhone and share access to Apple services, eligible purchases, iCloud storage, and more. with your family members, follow these steps:

1. **Go to the Shared Settings group:** Open the Settings app on your iPhone and tap your name at the top. Next, tap "Family Sharing".

2. **Start setting up Family Sharing:**
Follow the onscreen instructions to set up your Family Sharing group. You'll be prompted to add family members by inviting them to join you. You can add up to five other family members.

3. **Designate an adult family member:** When you add an adult family member, you can designate them as a parent or guardian, if applicable.

4. **Choose features to share:** Tap the features you want to set up for the

Family Sharing group, such as iCloud

storage, Apple subscriptions,

purchases, location, Apple Card, and

permissions Parental control. Follow

the on-screen instructions for each

feature.


5. **Set up parental controls:** If you're

setting up parental controls for a

child, tap the child's name, select the

feature you want to control, and follow

On-screen instructions for setting up

restrictions.

6. **Adjust sharing settings:** You can see what you share with your family and adjust sharing settings at any time by going to Settings > [your name] > Sharing in family.

7. **Explore Family Sharing features:** With Family Sharing, you can share passwords, iCloud Drive folders, subscriptions, purchases, locations, Apple Card , parental controls, and device configuration for children. Take advantage of these features to improve your family's digital experience.

8. **Using the Family Checklist:** You can use the Family Checklist feature in Settings > Family to review tips and recommendations for Family Sharing.

*By following these steps, you can easily set up and manage Family Sharing on iPhone, allowing you and your family members to enjoy shared access to services and features. Apple's various capabilities while maintaining control and security.*

# Add A Member to A Family Sharing Group

To add members to a Family Sharing group on your iPhone, follow these steps:

1. **Access Family Sharing settings:** Open the Settings app on your iPhone and tap "Family".

2. **Start adding members:** Tap the "Add members" button located in the upper right corner of the Family Sharing screen.

3. **Choose your invitation method:**
Tap "Invite others," then follow the
onscreen instructions.

4. **Send invitation:** Choose the
invitation sending method, which can
be AirDrop, Message or Mail.
Additionally, if a family member is
nearby, you can tap "Invite Directly"
and ask them to enter their Apple ID
and password on your device.

5. **Create an Apple ID for a child:** If
you're adding a child who doesn't have
their own Apple ID, follow these steps:

- Go to Settings > Family.

- Click the "Add member" button.

- Select "Create a child account" if you're the organizer, or just tap the "Add members" button if you're a parent or guardian.

- Follow the onscreen instructions to complete creating your child's Apple ID. You can set content limits, communication limits, and downtime, share their location with family, and turn on Ask to Buy.

6. **Complete setup:** Once the invitation is sent or the child's Apple ID is created, the new member will receive the invitation and can agree to join the Family Sharing group.

7. **Manage Family Sharing:** As the organizer or parent/guardian, you can manage Family Sharing settings, including content restrictions content, contact limits, location sharing, etc., from Family Sharing settings.

*By following these steps, you can easily add members to a Family Sharing group on iPhone, allowing you to share access*

*to various Apple services and features*

*with your family yourself while*

*maintaining privacy and control.*

# Set Up Parental Controls

To set up parental controls for children in a Family Sharing group on iPhone, follow these steps:

## Customize parental controls during setup:

1. 1 When you add a child to a Family Sharing group or when you set up a device for a child, follow the onscreen instructions.

2. Customize parental controls during setup, including age restrictions on app content, books, TV shows and movies, downtime, and limits on

specific apps, contact restrictions, and approval for free purchases or downloads.

3. You can change these settings at any time by going to Settings > Screen Time > [Child's Name] on your iPhone.

## Get warnings about sensitive content:

1. Screen Time can alert you if you or other members of your household receive or send sensitive content, including photos or videos.

2. You can block sensitive content and set purchase restrictions by going to Settings > Screen Time > Content & Privacy Restrictions on your iPhone.

## Set up screen time for the following children:

1. Go to Settings > Family > [Child's name] > Screen time.

2. Tap the child you want to set Screen Time for, then tap "Screen Time" and follow the onscreen instructions.

3. Manage settings for downtime, app usage, contacts, content ratings, and more.

**Enable Ask to buy later for your child:**

1. Go to Settings > Family > [Child's name].

2. Tap "Ask to Buy" and follow the on-screen instructions to set up Ask to Buy.

3. With Ask to Buy, a child's purchase must be approved by the family organizer or a parent or guardian in the family group.

# Set Up a Device for A Child

To set up a child's new iPhone or iPad
with Family Sharing on your iPhone, you
can use Quick Start or set it up manually
in Settings. Here's how:

## Use Quick Start to set up:

1. Make sure your iPhone is signed in
   with your Apple ID.
2. Turn on your new iPhone or iPad and
   hold down the Side button or Top
   button until the Apple logo appears.
3. Bring your iPhone closer to the new
   device.

4. When prompted on your iPhone, tap "Continue" and select your child's name in the Family Sharing group.

5. Follow the onscreen instructions to complete setup, including creating a new Apple ID for your child if needed.

## Installation without quick start:

1. Turn on the new device and select "Install without another device" when prompted.

2. Follow the onscreen instructions and select "Set up for children in my family. "

3. Continue setup when prompted.

## Set up in Settings:

1. If you're not signed in to your child's account during setup, go to Settings.

2. Tap "Connect to your iPhone" and select "Use another Apple device" or "Connect manually."

3. Follow the onscreen instructions to sign in with your child's Apple ID or create a new account for your child.

4. Continue the setup process, customizing content restrictions, communication limits, downtime, screen time settings, and more, if desired.

*By following these steps, you can easily set up a new iPhone or iPad for a child in your Family Sharing group and customize parental controls to ensure they have a digital home Safe, controlled.*

# SCREEN TIME ON IPHONE

To get started with Screen Time on iPhone and track device usage for you and your family members, follow these steps:

1. **Turn on Screen Time:**

   - Open Settings on your iPhone.

   - Scroll down and tap "Screen time".

   - Tap "App and website activity".

   - Tap "Enable app and website activity" to enable screen time tracking.

**2. Use Screen Time across all your devices:**

- To sync Screen Time settings and reports across all devices linked to your Apple ID, go back Prime Screen Time settings.

- Scroll down and enable "Share across devices".

**3. See a summary of your device usage:**

- When app and website activity is enabled, you can see a full report of your device usage.

- Go to Settings > Usage time.

- Tap "See all app and website activity".
- Select the device you want to see usage for.
- Choose between "Week" or "Day" to see a summary of your weekly or daily usage.

## 4. Use the Screen Time widget:

- You can add the Screen Time widget to your home screen for quick access to device usage information.
- Long press on the home screen to enter jiggle mode.

- Tap the "+" icon in the upper left corner to add a widget.
- Find and select the Screen Time widget.
- Choose the widget size that suits your preferences. - Place the widget on your home screen.
- Tap the widget to see detailed usage information, or select a family member's report if you've set up Screen Time for family sharing.

# Help protect your vision health

To protect your vision health, you can use the Screen Distance feature in Screen Time on your iPhone. How to activate it:

1. Open the Settings app on your iPhone.
2. Scroll down and tap Screen Time. "
3. Tap Screen Distance.
4. Enable the Screen Distance option.

Once Screen Distance is turned on, the TrueDepth camera (on supported models) is used to detect when you are using your iPhone Bring it closer to 12 inches over a longer period of time. When you do this,

Screen Distance will display an on-screen warning asking you to move the device further away to protect your eye health.

If you receive a screen distance warning:

- Move your iPhone further than 12 inches away.
- The Next button in the alert is activated.
- Tap Continue to continue using your iPhone.

*By using the screen removal feature, you can promote healthy viewing habits and reduce the risk of myopia in younger users, as well as reduce digital eye strain*

*for users of all ages.*

# Set Communication and Safety Limits

To protect your privacy and block inappropriate content using Screen Time on your iPhone, follow these steps:

## 1. Allow or block calls and messages from specific contacts:

- Make sure your contacts are with iCloud synced by going to Settings > [your name] > iCloud and turning on Contacts if it's not already turned on.

- Open the Settings app and tap Screen Time.

- Tap "Communication Restrictions" and select "During Screen Time."

- Select one of the following options:

  - **_Contacts Only:_** Allows you to communicate only with contacts in your address book.

  - **_Contacts and groups with at least one contact:_** Allow one-on-one conversations with people in your contacts and group conversations involving at least one person in your contacts.

  - **_Everyone:_** Allow conversations with anyone, even unknown numbers.

- Tap Back, then tap During Downtime.

- Select Specific Contacts to select contacts to allow communication with during downtime, or select Everyone to enable conversations with anyone.

## 2. Check for sensitive images:

- Go to Settings > Screen Time.

- Tap "Communication Security" and enable communications security.

- When enabled, iPhone will detect nude images before displaying them and display a warning if such content is detected.

## 3. Block inappropriate content:

- Go to Settings > Screen Time.

- Tap "Content & Privacy
  Restrictions" and enable "Content
  & Privacy Restrictions".

- You can set a password that is
  required before changing settings.

- Select options to set content
  quotas for iTunes Store and App
  Store purchases, app usage,
  content ratings, and more.

*By following these steps, you can use*
*Screen Time to help protect your privacy*

*and prevent inappropriate content from*

*appearing on your iPhone.*

# ACCESSORIES

**Charging cable for iPhone**

Your iPhone comes with one of two types

of charging cables:

## 1. USB-C Cable:

- This cable has a USB-C port on

   both ends.

- Allows you to connect your iPhone

   to a power outlet using a

   compatible power adapter (sold

   separately).

- It can also be connected to your computer's USB-C port for charging, file transfer and other functions.

## 2. USB-C to Lightning Cable:

- This cable has a USB-C connector on one end and a Lightning connector on the other end.
- Allows you to connect your iPhone to a power outlet using a compatible power adapter (sold separately).
- Like the USB-C cable, it can also be connected to your computer's

USB-C port for charging, file
transfer and more.

*Note:* Both cables are used to charge
your iPhone and facilitate data transfer.
However, the USB-C to Lightning cable is
specifically designed for use with devices
with a Lightning port, such as: iPhones,
iPads and some AirPods models.

# Power Adapters for iPhone

To charge your iPhone, you can use the included charging cable together with a compatible power adapter. These are the USB power adapters from Apple that you can use to charge your iPhone:

## 1. Apple 20W USB-C Power Adapter:

- This power adapter has a USB-C port.

- Provides fast charging for iPhone 12, iPhone SE (3rd generation) and newer models.

- Make sure the power supply you are using meets the following specifications:

- Frequency: 50 to 60 Hz, single phase

- Line voltage: 100 to 240 VAC

- Output voltage/current: 9 VDC/2. 2A

- Minimum output power: 20W

## 2. Apple 18W USB-C Power Adapter:

- Similar to the 20W adapter, but with slightly lower output power.

### 4. Apple 5W USB Power Adapter:

- This power adapter has a USB-A port.

- Provides standard charging for all iPhone models.

- Although it is slower than USB-C adapters, it is still enough to charge your iPhone.


*You can also use Apple USB power adapters designed for iPads and Mac laptops to charge your iPhone. In addition, third-party power supplies that comply with relevant safety standards and regulations can be used. Make sure any third-party adapters you use meet*

*the specifications required for safe and*

*efficient charging.*

# Qi-Certified Wireless Chargers

To charge your iPhone or AirPods wirelessly with a Qi-certified charger, follow these steps:

1. **Connect the charger to power:**

   Use the power adapter that came with your charger or a power adapter recommended by the manufacturer. Make sure the charger is connected to a power source.

2. **Place iPhone on charger:**

   - For iPhone: Place your iPhone face up in the center of the Qi-certified charger. Make sure your iPhone is properly aligned with the charger.

- Once aligned correctly, you should see the battery charging icon in the status bar, indicating that your iPhone is charging wirelessly.

3. **Charge AirPods with Wireless Charging Case:**

- If you have AirPods (2nd Generation) with Wireless Charging Case, AirPods (3rd Generation), or AirPods Pro, place the AirPods in the wireless charging case.

- Close the wireless charging case lid
tightly. - Then place the wireless
charging case in the middle of the
Qi-certified charger with the status
indicator facing up.

- When aligned correctly, the status
light on the wireless charging case
should illuminate for a few
seconds, indicating that charging
has begun. The status light may
then turn off while charging
continues.

*Note:* Make sure both your iPhone and
AirPods (if applicable) are properly

aligned with the Qi-certified charger to

ensure efficient charging.

# Use Airpods With iPhone

To pair your AirPods with your iPhone, follow these steps:

1. **Turn on Bluetooth:** Open the Settings app on your iPhone and tap "Bluetooth". Toggle the switch to enable Bluetooth if it is not already enabled.

2. **Prepare AirPods for pairing:**
   - For AirPods (1st, 2nd, and 3rd generations) and AirPods Pro: Open the case with your AirPods inside.

- For AirPods Max: Take your AirPods Max out of the Smart Case.

**3. Hold AirPods close to your iPhone:** Hold the opened AirPods case (or AirPods Max) close to your iPhone. The iPhone should detect the AirPods and display a message on the screen.

**4. Follow on-screen instructions:** Tap Connect or follow the on-screen instructions to complete the pairing process. After pairing is successful, tap Done.

**5. Automatic pairing between devices:** Your AirPods will now automatically pair with all Apple devices that you are signed in to with the same Apple ID.

# Use EarPods with iPhone

Follow these instructions to use EarPods with your iPhone:

## Control audio with your EarPods:

- Pause: Press the center button. Press again to resume playback.
- Jump forward: Quickly press the middle button twice.
- Jump back: Quickly press the middle button three times.
- Fast Forward: Quickly press and hold the center button twice.

## Manage calls with your EarPods:

- Answer incoming call: Press the center button.
- End the current call: Press the middle button.
- Switch to an incoming or waiting call and put the current call on hold: Press the center button. Press again to return to the first call.

**Ask Siri with your EarPods:**

- Press and hold the middle button until you hear a beep. Release the button and ask Siri to perform a task or answer your question.

# Use Apple Watch with iPhone

## Pair Apple Watch with iPhone:

- Open the Apple Watch app on your
  iPhone, then follow the on-screen
  instructions to pair your Apple
  Watch to pair.

## Unlock iPhone with Apple Watch:

- On your iPhone, go to Settings >
  Face ID & Password.
- Scroll down and turn on Apple
  Watch under Unlock with Apple
  Watch.

## Work out with Apple Fitness+:

- Apple Fitness+ is a subscription service that offers a variety of workouts led by expert trainers. It works in conjunction with Apple Watch and displays metrics like heart rate and calories burned on your iPhone screen during the session.

## Collects health and fitness data from Apple Watch:

- Apple Watch sends health and fitness data to your iPhone, which you can view in the Health app. It

also sends notifications to your

iPhone about high or low heart

rates, loud ambient noise, and

more.

# Apple TV, Smart TV and videos Display

## Wirelessly stream videos and photos

To stream videos or photos from iPhone to an Apple TV or Smart TV that supports AirPlay 2, follow these steps:

### *Play videos on an Apple TV or Smart TV that supports AirPlay 2:*

1.  While if you're watching a video in the Apple TV app or other supported video app on your iPhone, tap the screen to show the controls.
2.  Press the AirPlay button.

3. Select Apple TV or an AirPlay 2-enabled smart TV as your playback destination.

4. If prompted, enter the AirPlay passcode displayed on your iPhone TV screen.

5. You can change the playback destination by selecting a different AirPlay option on the iPhone screen.

## *View photos on Apple TV or Smart TV that supports AirPlay 2:*

1. Open the Photos app on your iPhone.

2. Click on the photo you want to view.

3. Click the Share button.

4. Swipe up then tap the AirPlay button.

5. Select Apple TV or an AirPlay 2-enabled smart TV as the playback destination.

6. If necessary, enter the AirPlay passcode displayed on your iPhone TV screen.

7. To stop streaming photos, tap the AirPlay button on your iPhone screen, then select "Turn AirPlay Off."

## Turn AirPlay auto-streaming on or off:

1. Go to Settings > General > AirPlay & Transfer on your iPhone.

2. Select "Auto," "Never," or "Ask" to control whether your iPhone automatically connects to your Apple TV or frequently used Smart TV when playing content via AirPlay.

### *Mirror your iPhone screen to an Apple TV or Smart TV:*

1. Open Control Center on your iPhone by swiping down from the upper right corner on iPhone models with Face ID or using by swiping up from the bottom of the screen. screen on iPhone models with a Home button.
2. Press the Screen mirroring button.

3. Select your Apple TV or AirPlay 2-enabled smart TV from the list of available devices.

4. If prompted, enter the AirPlay passcode displayed on your iPhone TV screen.

5. To stop mirroring, open Control Center again, tap the Screen mirroring button, then select "Stop mirroring."

*With these steps, you can easily stream videos and photos from your iPhone to your Apple TV or AirPlay 2-enabled smart TV, and mirror your iPhone screen if needed.*

## Connect iPhone to A Display with A Cable

1. Depends your iPhone model, plug in Lightning Digital AV. Adapter, Lightning to VGA Adapter, USB-C Display AV Adapter, or USB-C VGA Multiport Adapter to the charging port on the bottom of your iPhone.

2. Connect the HDMI or VGA cable to the appropriate port on the adapter.

3. Connect the other end of the HDMI or VGA cable to a monitor, TV, or projector.

4. If necessary, switch to the correct video source on the monitor, TV, or projector using the remote control or menu options.

5. Adapters often have an additional port so you can simultaneously connect a charging cable to charge your iPhone while connected to a display.

# External Storage Device

## Connect an external storage device to iPhone:

1. Connect a USB flash drive or SD card reader to the iPhone's charging port using a compatible connector or adapter.

2. You may need Lightning to USB Camera Adapter, Lightning to USB 3 Camera Adapter, USB-C to SD Camera Reader, or Lightning to SD Camera Reader (all sold separately).

3. Insert the SD memory card into the card reader, making sure the card is inserted properly.

4. To view the contents of the drive or memory card, open a supported application such as Files. Tap "Browse" at the bottom of the screen, then tap the device name under "Locations." If you don't see "Locations," tap "Browse" again at the bottom of the screen.

5. To disconnect the reader or card reader, simply remove it from the iPhone's charging port.

*Note:* External hard drives typically require an external power source when used with iPhone. If your external hard drive isn't self-powered, you can use a

powered USB hub for your iPhone that

has a USB-C connector. If your iPhone

has a Lightning connector, you can use

the Lightning to USB 3 Camera Adapter

connected to a USB power adapter for

power.

# Bluetooth Accessory

To set up and use a Bluetooth accessory on iPhone, follow these steps:

## Pair a Bluetooth device:

1. Put the Bluetooth device into discovery or pairing mode according to the instructions of device.

2. On your iPhone, go to Settings > Bluetooth, then turn on Bluetooth.

3. Tap the Bluetooth device name when it appears in the list of available devices.

4. Follow the on-screen prompts to complete the pairing process.

## Customize your wireless game controller:

1. After pairing a compatible game controller, go to Settings > General > Game Controllers on your iPhone.
2. Tap the buttons you want to customize.
3. To customize a specific app, tap "Add app".

## Play iPhone audio to a Bluetooth audio device:

1. Open an audio app on your iPhone, such as Music.
2. Select the item to play.

3. Press the "Play Destination" button.

4. Select your Bluetooth device from the list.

5. You can change the playback destination on the lock screen or in control center during audio playback.

**Improved audio accuracy of third-party Bluetooth devices:**

1. Go to Settings > Bluetooth.

2. Tap the "Available Operations" button next to the device name.

3. Tap "Device type" and select the appropriate device type.

**Skip your Bluetooth device to make a call:**

1. Answer the call by tapping the iPhone screen.

2. During a call, tap "Audio," then select "iPhone" or "Speaker Phone."

3. You can also turn off the Bluetooth device, unpair it, or move it out of range.

**Disconnect Bluetooth device:**

1. Go to Settings > Bluetooth.

2. Press the information button next to the device name.

3. Tap "Forget this device".

## Disconnect a Bluetooth device:

To quickly disconnect from all Bluetooth devices without turning off Bluetooth, open Control Center, then press the Bluetooth button.

*Follow these steps to set up, customize, and effectively use Bluetooth accessories with your iPhone, if you encounter problems.*

# Print From iPhone

To print from iPhone using AirPrint, follow these steps:

## 1. Ensure compatibility and connectivity:

- Make sure your printer is compatible with AirPrint and connected to the same network Wi-Fi with your iPhone.

## 2. Check print job status:

- Open App Switcher (by swiping up from the bottom of the screen and holding), then tap "Print Center. "

- The badge on the Print Center icon will indicate the number of documents in the print queue.

- To cancel a print job, select the print job in the Print Center, then press "Cancel Print"

## 3. Print documents:

- Open the document or image you want to print in an app like Mail, Photos, Safari or any other supported app

- Tap the Share button (it looks like a square with an arrow pointing up), the More button (three dots), the Reply button (if available), or the Action Menu button (depending on the app).

- Find the option labeled "Print" and tap on it. If you don't see the Print option, swipe up on the share sheet to see more options.

- Your iPhone will detect nearby AirPrint-enabled printers. Select the printer you want to use.

- Adjust print settings as needed, such as number of copies, paper size, or color options.

- Finally click "Print" to send the document to the printer.

*By following these steps, you can easily print documents, photos, web pages, and more directly from iPhone using AirPrint.*

# USE IPHONE WITH IPAD, MAC, AND PC

To use your iPhone with other devices such as an iPad, Mac, or PC, you can share your iPhone's internet connection using Personal Hotspot. Here's how to set it up and connect your devices:

1. **Set up Personal Hotspot on iPhone:**
   - Go to Settings > Cellular.
   - Tap on "Set Up Personal Hotspot" and follow the on-screen instructions.

- If you don't see the option for
Personal Hotspot, make sure
Cellular Data is turned on and
contact your carrier if needed to
add Personal Hotspot to your plan.

## 2. Connect your Mac or PC to your Personal Hotspot:

You can use Wi-Fi, USB, or Bluetooth to
connect your Mac or PC.

### - For Wi-Fi:

- On your Mac or PC, find Wi-Fi
settings and select the Personal
Hotspot network on your iPhone.
- Enter password if prompted.

### - For USB:

- Connect your iPhone to your Mac or PC using a USB cable.
- Your Mac or PC will automatically detect your iPhone Personal Hotspot and establish a connection.

### - For Bluetooth:

- Follow the manufacturer's instructions to set up a Bluetooth network connection between iPhone and your Mac or PC.

## 3. Connect another iPad or iPhone to your Personal Hotspot:

- On the other device, go to Settings > Wi-Fi

- Select the Personal Hotspot network on your iPhone in the list of available networks.

- Enter your Personal Hotspot password if prompted.

## 4. Turn off Personal Hotspot or change your password:

- Go to Settings > Personal Hotspot on your iPhone.

- To change the password, tap "Wi-Fi Password" and follow the on-screen instructions.

- To turn off Personal Hotspot, turn off the "Allow others to join" option. This will disconnect all devices using your personal hotspot.

## 4. Monitor your mobile data usage:

- To monitor mobile data usage while sharing a personal hotspot, go to Settings > Cellular on your iPhone.

## Allow phone calls on your iPad and Mac

To make and receive phone calls on your iPad, Mac, or another iPhone through your iPhone, you can set up call forwarding. Here's how:

**Before you begin:**

Make sure your device meets the following requirements:

- Requires iOS 9, iPadOS 13, or macOS 10. 10 or later.
- FaceTime must be configured on all devices.
- Sign in to all devices with the same Apple ID.

**Allow calls to other devices from iPhone:**

**1. On your iPhone:**

- Go to Settings > Mobile.

- If your iPhone has two SIM cards, select one line (under SIM).

- Tap "Calls on other devices" and enable "Allow calls on other devices".

- Select the device you want to make and receive calls.

- You can also tap "Wi-Fi Calling," turn on "Wi-Fi Calling on this iPhone," then turn on "Add Wi-Fi calling for other devices."

**2. On your other devices (iPad, iPhone, or Mac):**

- On iPad or iPhone: Go to Settings > FaceTime and turn on FaceTime.

- On Mac: Open FaceTime, choose FaceTime > Settings, then select "Calls from iPhone." If prompted, click "Upgrade to Wi-Fi Calling" and follow the instructions.

**Make or receive a phone call:**

- *Make a call:* Tap or click a phone number in Contacts, Calendar, FaceTime, Messages, Search, or Safari. You can also open FaceTime, enter a contact or phone number, then tap the FaceTime Audio button.

- ***Receive a call:*** Swipe, tap or click the notification to answer or ignore the call.

**Additional notes:**

- When you make a call from another device via call forwarding, it will use your voice line by default if dual SIM is enabled.

- If you turn on Wi-Fi calling, emergency calls can be made over Wi-Fi and location information on your device can be used for emergency calls to assist with

support response efforts, whether

or not you have location services

turned on.

# Connect iPhone and Your Computer with A Cable

To connect your iPhone directly to a Mac with iPhone OS charging, connect your iPhone to a USB port on your computer. Make sure the USB port is compatible with the cable. If not, you may need to use an adapter (sold separately).

1. **Trust this computer:**

   - If a warning appears on your iPhone asking whether you should trust this computer, select "Trust". This step is important to establish a secure connection between your

iPhone and computer.

## 2. Perform various tasks:

After you connect iPhone to your

computer with a cable, you can perform

various tasks:

- Set up iPhone for the first time.

- Share iPhone's Internet

  connection with computer.

- Use a computer to delete all

  content and settings on iPhone.

- Update iPhone using computer.

- Sync content or transfer files

  between your Mac and iPhone.

- Sync or transfer files between your PC and iPhone.

## 3. Charging:

- When iPhone is connected to your computer and your computer is connected to a power source, the iPhone battery charges. This allows you to charge your iPhone while performing other tasks or transferring data.

# Transfer Files

To transfer files between your iPhone and your computer, you have several options:

1. **Use AirDrop:** With AirDrop you can quickly transfer photos, videos, and other files wirelessly between your iPhone and nearby Apple devices. Simply enable AirDrop on both devices and follow the instructions to share items.

2. **Use iCloud:** iCloud enables seamless file syncing between your Apple devices. Enabling iCloud Drive allows you to access your files from any

device connected to your iCloud account. This ensures that your files are always up to date.

3. **Use external storage or cloud services:** You can use external storage devices, file servers, or cloud storage services such as Box or Dropbox to transfer files between your iPhone and your computer. Simply upload the files to the cloud service or connect the external storage device to your iPhone and transfer the files.

4. **Use a cable (Mac and PC):**

- **_For Mac:_** You can use iTunes or Finder to sync files between your Mac and iPhone. Connect your iPhone to your Mac using a USB cable and follow the instructions to sync files.
- **_For PC:_** You can also use iTunes to transfer files between your PC and iPhone. Connect your iPhone to your PC via a USB cable and manage your files with iTunes.

*It is important to note that transfer, sharing or synchronization may be restricted for certain types of data, such as: for files saved in proprietary formats, older software versions or copyrighted files. Be sure to check the restrictions and compatibility of the files you want to transfer.*

**To transfer files using an external storage device, file server, or cloud storage service to your iPhone, follow these steps:**

1. **Transfer files using an external storage device:**
   - Connect your iPhone or computer to an external storage device such

as a USB stick or SD card. You may need a cable adapter to connect the storage device to iPhone.

- Use a supported app like Files or Pages to copy files to your iPhone storage device.

- Disconnect the storage device and connect it to the device you want the copied files to appear on. Next, copy the files to the connected device using the method appropriate for your computer system.

**2. Transfer files using a file server:**

- Set up your Mac as a file server on your local network if you haven't done so already.

- Connect to a file server from your iPhone using the Files app.

- Connect your Mac or PC to the file server.

- Use File Server to transfer files between iPhone and your computer. Once done, disconnect your iPhone from the file server.

**3. Transfer files using a cloud storage service like Box or Dropbox:**

- Follow the instructions provided by the cloud storage service on your iPhone or computer to download the files you want to share.
- To access your shared files on iPhone, open the Files app, tap Browse, then tap the storage service name under Locations.
- To access files shared on your computer, follow the instructions provided by the cloud storage service.

*Note:* some methods may require a subscription fee, especially for cloud storage services. Make sure you choose the method that best suits your needs and preferences for transferring files between your devices.

# Automatically Keep Your Files Up to Date

To automatically update your files on iPhone and computer using iCloud, follow these steps:

1.  **Set up iCloud on iPhone:**

    -   Open the Settings app on your iPhone.

    -   Tap your name at the top of the screen.

    -   If you're not signed in, tap "Sign in to your iPhone" and enter your Apple ID and password.

- Tap "iCloud" and enable items you want to sync with iCloud, such as iCloud Drive for your files.

## 2. Set up iCloud on your Mac:

- Enable the same things you enabled for your iPhone, make sure iCloud Drive is enabled to sync your files.

## 3. Set up iCloud on your PC:

- Enable the same items you enabled for your iPhone, then press Apply to apply the changes.

*By setting up iCloud on your device, files, photos, videos, and more will be stored in iCloud, allowing you to access and sync them across all your devices. Any changes made to files on one device automatically appear on all devices signed in to iCloud with the same Apple ID.*

**Note:** Some iCloud features require minimum system requirements and iCloud availability may vary by region. Additionally, you can sign up for iCloud+ to get more storage and additional features beyond the 5GB of free storage

that comes with iCloud.

# IPHONE CARPLAY

To connect your iPhone to CarPlay and use its features, follow these steps:

1.  **Connect iPhone to CarPlay:**

- Start your car and ensure Siri has been enabled.

- Connect iPhone to your car using one of the following methods:

    -   If your car supports CarPlay using a USB cable: Plug your iPhone into your car's USB port using an Apple USB cable.

- If your car supports wired and wireless CarPlay: Plug your iPhone into your car's USB port. The next time you log in, you will have the option to connect wirelessly.

- If your car only supports wireless CarPlay: Press and hold the voice control button on the steering wheel, make sure your stereo is in wireless or Bluetooth mode, and make sure Wi-Fi is turned on in settings Place on your iPhone. Select the CarPlay network in Wi-Fi settings, make sure automatic connection is turned on, and select your car in Settings > General >

CarPlay.

- On some car models, CarPlay

  Home appears automatically when

  you connect your iPhone. If not,

  select the CarPlay logo on your

  car's screen.

## 2. Use Siri to control CarPlay:

- Activate Siri by pressing and

  holding the voice control button on

  the steering wheel or pressing and

  holding the Home/CarPlay

  Dashboard button on the

  touchscreen.

- Use Siri to perform a variety of tasks like getting directions, making calls, listening to music, checking the weather, setting reminders, and more.

## 3. Change settings in CarPlay:

- Open settings in CarPlay using your car's built-in controller.

- Customize CarPlay settings, such as changing the wallpaper, enabling driving focus, switching between dark and light interface, showing or hiding suggestions in

the dashboard, and showing or
hiding cover art album.

## 4. Use Driving Focus with CarPlay:

- Enable Driving Focus to stay
  focused on the road when
  connected to CarPlay. This feature
  mutes or limits notifications and
  text messages.
- Activate Driving Focus by opening
  settings in CarPlay and selecting
  "Activate with CarPlay".

*Note:* If you receive a Focus on Driving
notification when you're not driving, you

can turn it off by tapping the notification

and selecting "I'm not driving."

# ACCESSIBILITY

## Get Started

To start using accessibility features on your iPhone, follow these steps:

1. **Explore Accessibility Settings:** Go to your iPhone's Settings and tap "Accessibility". Here you'll find a range of features categorized by vision, mobility, hearing, speech and cognitive needs.


2. **Visibility:** Adjust screen color, text size, and zoom settings to improve visibility. You can also turn on

VoiceOver to have your iPhone read the content on the screen aloud.

3. **Mobile:** Customize gestures, connect external input devices like a switch or mouse, and adjust touch sensitivity to navigate your iPhone more easily.

4. **Hearing:** Adjust audio settings for noisy environments, enable live captions to display text for spoken content, or configure alerts for clearer display.

5. **Speech:** Use communication features, such as voice commands or dictation, to interact with iPhone using your voice.

6. **Awareness:** Reduce distractions, get help with tasks like entering or logging into accounts, and simplify interactions with targeted choices.

7. **Access to Support:** Allows people with cognitive disabilities to have access to support to complete common tasks while reducing cognitive load.

8. **Turn on accessibility features:**
Use Siri to turn on accessibility
features with voice commands like
"Turn on VoiceOver" or "Turn off
VoiceOver". You can also add
accessibility features to Control Center
for quick access.

*By exploring and configuring these
accessibility features, you can adjust
your iPhone to better meet your needs
and make it easier to use, whether
temporarily or continuously.*

# Turn On Accessibility Features

To turn on accessibility features when you first set up iPhone, follow these steps:

1. **VoiceOver:** Triple-click the side button (on iPhone with Face ID) or triple-click Home button (on other iPhone models) to activate VoiceOver. VoiceOver provides spoken feedback to describe what's happening on the screen. You can explore and interact with items by touching the screen or using gestures.

2. **Zoom:** Double-tap the screen with three fingers to activate zoom. You can adjust the magnification level with the slider and navigate the magnification screen with a simple three-finger swipe.

3. **Accessibility options:** During initial setup, tap the "Accessibility options" button to access additional accessibility features:
   - *VoiceOver:* Customize VoiceOver settings such as language, voice, speaking speed, and level of detail.
   - *Zoom:* Adjust zoom settings.

- *Display and Text Size:* Change display and text size settings to make content easier to read.

- *Motion:* Configure settings related to motion sensitivity.

- *Speech:* Enable speech for selected items.

- *Touch:* Access additional touch features such as Assistive Touch, Touch Assist, and Switch Control.

4. **Quick Start:** If you've already set up accessibility features on another iPhone or iPad nearby, you can transfer your settings to your new

iPhone using Quick Start. Follow the onscreen instructions to switch accessibility settings seamlessly.

*By turning on these accessibility features during setup, you can personalize your iPhone experience to better meet your needs and preferences from the start.*

# Set Up Hearing-Related Accessibility Features

To set up hearing-related accessibility features on your iPhone, follow these steps:

1. **Turn audio into text:**

    - *Sound recognition:* This feature alerts you to specific sounds like alarms, doorbells, etc.

    - *Live Captions (beta):* Live Captions displays captions for media playing on your iPhone, including video and audio messages.

- **_RTT and TTY:_** Real-time messaging and Teletype allow you to communicate by entering text during a phone call.

## 2. Hear Better in Different Situations:

- **_MFi Hearing Devices:_** Pair Made for iPhone (MFi) hearing aids or sound processors with your iPhone to adjust their settings and improve your hearing experience.
- **_AirPods:_** Use AirPods or other compatible Bluetooth headphones

for personalized audio experiences.

- *Live Listen:* Use Live Listen to stream audio from your iPhone's microphone to your hearing aids or AirPods to enhance hearing in challenging environments.

- *Audio Settings:* Adjust Phone Noise Cancellation and Conversation Boost to tailor audio settings to your preferences.

## 3. Write down your alerts:

- *LED flash for alerts:* Enable LED flash notifications for

incoming calls, messages and
alerts.

- *Vibration:* Set vibration alerts
  for notifications and incoming
  calls.

- *Siri Notification
  Notifications:* Asks Siri to
  announce notifications, providing
  audible alerts for various events.

## 4. Configure and use RTT and TTY:

- *RTT and TTY:* Enable RTT/TTY
  software for SMS communication
  during phone calls. Hardware TTY
  support is also available for

connection to external TTY devices.

- ***Connect iPhone to an external TTY device:*** Use the iPhone TTY adapter to connect your iPhone to an external TTY device for text communications.

- ***Start an RTT or TTY call:*** Start or accept an RTT or TTY call from the Phone app and enter text messages during the call.

- ***View RTT or TTY call records:*** Access RTT or TTY call records in the Phone app to view the conversation.

To access these features, go to Settings > Accessibility on your iPhone and explore the Hearing section. From here, you can customize settings, pair your hearing aids, enable RTT/TTY, and configure audio options to enhance your listening experience.

# PRIVACY AND SECURITY

## Take Advantage of iPhone's Built-In Security and Privacy Features

iPhone is designed to protect your data and privacy. Its built-in security features limit access to your information, allowing you to customize sharing preferences. Additionally, built-in security measures prevent unauthorized access to your iPhone and iCloud data.

To take full advantage of these security and privacy features, follow these guidelines:

## Device Access Protection

- Implement a secure passcode
- Use Face ID or Touch ID to authenticate
- Enable Find My iPhone to Protect yourself from loss or theft
- Manage access to features when your device is locked
- Use stolen device protection for added security

## Protect your Apple ID

- Protect your Apple ID, to protect your data

## Improve account sign-ins

- Simplify password sign-ins or sign in with Apple.
- Allow iPhone to generate strong passwords for added security.
- Share passcodes and passwords securely with AirDrop.
- Use the built-in authenticator for two-factor authentication.
- Easily complete SMS passcodes for hassle-free verification

- Keep passwords updated across devices with iCloud Keychain.

## Management Data Sharing

- Use Security Checkup to verify shared information and update.
- Control app tracking permissions and data sharing.
- Review and adjust data sharing settings with apps
- Evaluate app privacy practices using the App Privacy Report

## Email privacy

- Enable email privacy to hide email activity
- Personal Protect your email address with the Hide My Email feature

## Ensure safe web browsing

- Improve online privacy with iCloud Private Relay.
- Use Safari's privacy features to avoid tracking and malicious websites.

## Defend yourself against cyberattacks.

- Enable lockdown mode for extreme security against sophisticated cyberattacks

# Set A Passcode on iPhone

Improve the security of your iPhone by setting a passcode. This adds a layer of protection that requires input to unlock your device, ensuring your data is protected. Follow these steps to set or change your passcode:

1. **Go to Passcode Settings:**

   - Go to Settings on your iPhone.

   - Depending on your device model, select "Face ID & Passcode" or "Touch ID & Passcode". "

2. **Set or change a passcode:**

- Tap "Enable passcode" or "Change passcode".

- To customize your passcode, tap "Passcode options" and choose from options such as custom alphanumeric passcode or custom numeric passcode

### 3. Use Face ID or Touch ID:

- On supported models, you can use Face ID or Touch ID to unlock. However, for added security, you should always enter your password in specific situations, such as device restart or long periods of

inactivity.

## 4. Adjust Auto-Lock settings:

- To control when your iPhone

  automatically locks, go to Settings

  > Display & Brightness > Auto-

  Lock and choose an interval you

  want.

## 5. Enable data deletion:

- Enable option to delete all data

  after 10 consecutive failed

  password attempts. This can be

done in Settings > Face ID &

Passcode or Touch ID & Passcode.

## 6. Disable or reset passcode:

- To turn off passcode, go to Settings

  > Face ID & Passcode or Touch ID

  & Passcode and tap "Turn off

  Passcode access".

- If you forget your password, see

  Apple Support for recovery

  options.

## Set up Face ID or Touch ID

Use Face ID or Touch ID for seamless

and secure authentication on your

iPhone. Here's how to set up these features:

1. **Set up Face ID:**

   - Go to Settings > Face ID & Passcode.

   - Follow the onscreen instructions to set up Face ID or add another interface if needed.

2. **Use Face ID with a mask:**

   - On compatible models, set Face ID to work with a mask through Settings > Face ID & Passcode.

3. **Temporarily turn off:**

- Temporarily turn off Face ID by pressing and holding the side button and volume button, then press the side button again to lock the device.

## 4. Turn off Face ID:

- In Settings > Face ID & Passcode, turn off Face ID for specific features or reset it completely if needed.

## Set up Touch ID

Enable Touch ID to quickly and securely access your iPhone. Follow these steps to set up Touch ID:

1. **Enable fingerprint recognition:**

   - Go to Settings > Touch ID & Passcode and follow the prompts to turn on fingerprint recognition.

2. **Add fingerprint:**

   - In the same settings, tap "Add fingerprint" and follow the instructions to add more fingerprints if you want.

3. **Manage Touch ID:**

- Customize Touch ID settings or turn it off completely from Settings > Touch ID & Passcode.

## Control access to the lock screen

Manage access to features from the lock screen to balance convenience and security. Go to Settings > Face ID & Passcode or Touch ID & Passcode to adjust these settings to your preferences.

# Protect Your browsing with iCloud Private Relay

Signing up for iCloud+ lets you use iCloud Private Relay, improving your online privacy by blocking sites and providers The network creates detailed profile information about you. Here's how to turn on iCloud Private Relay and manage its settings:

1. **Turn on iCloud Private Relay:**

   - Go to Settings > [Your name] > iCloud > Private Relay.

   - Tap "Individual Relay" to turn it on.

*Note:* you must enable iCloud Private Relay on each device you want to use.

## 2. Turn off iCloud Private Forwarding:

- Follow the same path to Settings > [Your Name] > iCloud > Private Forwarding.

- Tap "Individual Relay" and select "Disable Individual Relay" to turn it off completely.

- You can also select "Off until tomorrow" to temporarily turn off iCloud Private Relay, which will automatically re-enable within 24 hours.

## 3. Manage iCloud Private Relay for Wi-Fi and cellular networks:

- For Wi-Fi networks, go to Settings > Wi-Fi, tap "Available tasks" and turn on "Limit by track IP address" to control iCloud Private. Relay.

- For cellular networks, go to Settings > Cellular > Cellular Data Options (or select one line for devices with multiple lines) and adjust "Limit IP Address Tracking" accordingly fit.

## 4. Customize IP address location settings:

- Fine-tune the specifics of your IP address location by going to Settings > [Your Name] > iCloud > Transfer private > IP address location.

- Choose between "Keep general location" to access local content or "Use country and time zone" for enhanced privacy.

*By following these steps, you can effectively protect your browsing activities and maintain greater control over your online privacy with iCloud Private Relay on iPhone.*

# Using A Private Network Address

Your iPhone uses a unique private network address, called a Media Access Control (MAC) address, for each Wi-Fi network on which it connects to, improve your privacy and security. However, there are situations where you may need to disable this feature, such as when the network requires your device to use a specific MAC address for authentication or parental controls. Here's how to manage private network addresses:

1. **Disable private network addresses:**

- Open settings and tap "Wi-Fi".

- Locate the network you want to
  disable private addresses for and
  tap that network's settings button.

- Switch the "Private address"
  switch to the off position.

## 2. Important note:

- You should enable the private
  address feature for networks that
  support it to improve your privacy.

- Using a private address helps
  minimize tracking of your iPhone
  across different Wi-Fi networks,

contributing to better privacy

protection.

# Use Advanced Data Protection for Your iCloud Data

By default, iCloud keeps your information safe by encrypting it during transmission as well as at rest and backup encryption keys in Apple data centers. Additionally, many Apple services use end-to-end encryption, where your data is encrypted with keys taken from your device and your device passcode, known only to you.

For maximum cloud data security, you can turn on Advanced Data Protection (requires iOS 16. 2 or later). This feature uses end-to-end encryption for additional

categories of data, including:

- Device backup

- Message backup

- iCloud Drive

- Notes

- Photos

- Reminders

- Safari Favorites

- Siri Shortcuts

- Voice Memos

- Wallet pass

With Advanced Data Protection, your

protected data can only be decrypted on

trusted devices, ensures your information

is secure even in the event of a cloud data breach. Notably, not even Apple can access your information.

## To enable advanced data protection features:

1. Go to Settings > [Your name] > iCloud.
2. Tap Advanced Data Protection.
3. Select Enable enhanced data protection.
4. If you haven't set up a recovery contact or recovery key, tap Account recovery, then set up account recovery

by following the onscreen
instructions.

**WARNING:** Enabling Advanced Data
Protection means taking responsibility for
data recovery. Since Apple doesn't have
the key needed to restore data, you must
set up a recovery contact or recovery key
on your account. These additional
recovery methods ensure access to your
data in case you forget your password or
lose account access.

If you later decide to turn off Advanced Data Protection, your iCloud data will return to the standard level of security.

# Protect Your iPhone Against Cyberattacks with Lockdown Mode

Lockdown Mode is an advanced security feature designed to protect your iPhone against sophisticated cyberthreats. It offers strict protections, including advanced wireless connection settings, secure media management, default media sharing restrictions, sandboxing, and network security optimization.

However, it should be noted that Lockdown Mode is an optional feature for users who consider themselves potential targets of advanced cyberattacks, such as those launched by private entity is developing state-sponsored spyware.

*Note:* Most individuals are unlikely to encounter such targeted attacks.

When Lock Mode is enabled on your iPhone, its functionality is significantly limited for added security. Some apps, websites, and features are strictly limited, and some features are disabled, including:

- SharePlay
- Shared Albums

- Live Photos in FaceTime

- Continuous Streaming in

  FaceTime

Additionally, in Locked mode, your

iPhone needs to be unlocked to connect to

wired accessories. (Limited connections

may be allowed for a short time after

enabling Locked Mode.)

## Enable Locked Mode:

1. Go to Settings > Privacy & Security >

   Lock mode.

2. Tap Enable Lock Mode.

If you have your Apple Watch set up with

your iPhone, turning on Locked Mode will

also enable the feature on the paired
Apple Watch (requires watchOS 10 or
later).

*Note:* For complete protection, make
sure lock mode is enabled on all your
devices.

# Use Stolen Device Protection

With iOS 17. 3 or later, Stolen Device Protection provides an additional layer of security against potential theft scenarios where a hacker The criminal knows your iPhone passcode. This feature minimizes risk by enforcing biometric authentication (Face ID or Touch ID) without the need for a password option.

When Stolen Device Protection is enabled, sensitive activities on the device and Apple ID account, such as changing the device passcode or Apple ID password, will require biometric authentication using Face ID or Touch ID, then security lag. This delay involves one successful biometric authentication, one hour of waiting, and then another successful biometric authentication. The security timeout prevents unauthorized people from making changes that could compromise your iPhone account or Apple ID. Plus, it gives you enough time to turn on Lost Mode using Find My or Find My Device on iCloud. com.

**Enable Stolen Device Protection:**

1. Go to Settings.

2. Depending on your iPhone model:

   - On an iPhone with Face ID: Tap
     Face ID & Passcode (enter your
     passcode if prompted).

   - On an iPhone with a Home button:
     Tap Touch ID & Passcode (enter
     your passcode if prompted).

3. Scroll down and select Protect stolen
   device.

4. If necessary, set up Face ID or Touch
   ID first.

5. Enable Stolen device protection.

6. Choose the right option based on your
   preferences:

   - Away from familiar locations: Use
     your device's anti-theft feature

when you're away from home or
work.

- Always: Use Stolen Device
Protection everywhere.

## Turn off stolen device protection:

1. Go to Setting.

2. Depending on your iPhone model:

   - On an iPhone with Face ID: Tap
     Face ID & Passcode (enter your
     passcode if prompted).

   - On an iPhone with a Home button:
     Tap Touch ID & Passcode (enter
     your passcode if prompted).

3. Scroll down and select Protect stolen device.

4. Turn off Stolen Device Protection.

5. If Stolen Device Protection is set to Away from home or Always and you are not at home or at work, you are required to set a protection timeout password to turn off this feature. Tap Start Security Timeout, then follow the onscreen instructions.

# Get Warnings About Sensitive Content

You can enable your iPhone to check for sensitive images and give you a warning before viewing them. This feature can be especially helpful in protecting you or your family members from potentially inappropriate content.

## Warning about enabling sensitive content:

1. Open Settings on your iPhone.
2. Tap Privacy and security.
3. Scroll down and find Sensitive Content Warning.

4. Turn on the switch to enable Sensitive Content Warning. Once enabled, you (or your designated family member) will receive a warning before sending or receiving sensitive images.

*Note:* If you have Screen Time set up and Communications Security turned on, Sensitive Content Warning is automatically turned on for added protection.

# RESTART, UPDATE, RESET, RESTORE, AND ERASE IPHONE

**Turn iPhone On or Off:**

- To turn on your iPhone, press and hold the side button until the Apple logo appears.

- To turn off your iPhone:

  - For iPhones with Face ID, simultaneously press and hold the side button and either volume button until the sliders appear.

Then, drag the Power Off slider.

- For iPhones with the Home

button, press and hold the side

button, then drag the slider.

- Alternatively, go to Settings >

General > Shut Down, then drag

the slider.

**Force Restart iPhone:**

If your iPhone is unresponsive and you

can't turn it off and on again, try force

restarting:

- Press and quickly release the
  Power button to increase the
  volume.

- Press and quickly release the
  volume down button.

- Press and hold the side button.

- When the Apple logo appears,
  release the side button.

## Update iOS on iPhone:

- Go to Settings > General >
  Software Update to check for
  updates.

- If an update is available, follow the on-screen instructions to download and install it.
- You can also update your iPhone using a computer by connecting it and using Finder or iTunes.

## Back up iPhone:

You can back up iPhone using iCloud or a computer. Here's how:

- *iCloud Backup:* Go to Settings > [your name] > iCloud > iCloud Backup and turn it on. Tap Back Up Now to manually back up your iPhone.

- ***Backup to computer:*** Connect iPhone to computer, then use Finder or iTunes to back up.

**Reset iPhone:**

If your iPhone has problems, you can reset:

- Go to Settings > General > Change or reset iPhone > Reset.
- Select the type of reset you want, such as Reset All Settings or Erase All Content and Settings.
- Follow the on-screen instructions to confirm your action.

**Restore iPhone:**

You can restore your iPhone from a backup to set it up as new or transfer your data:

- *From an iCloud backup:* During setup , select Restore from iCloud Backup and follow the instructions.

- *From a computer backup:* Connect your iPhone to your computer and use Finder or iTunes to restore the device from the backup.

**Erase iPhone:**

If you want to erase all content and settings on iPhone:

- Go to Settings > General > Transfer or reset iPhone > Erase all content and settings.
- Follow the on-screen instructions to confirm your action.

*Taking these actions can help you fix problems, update your iPhone, and ensure your data is backed up and secure.*

# Install Or Remove Configuration Profiles

To install or remove a configuration profile on iPhone, follow these steps:

## Install a configuration profile:

1. Open the email or website containing the configuration profile.

2. Click the configuration profile file. You may be asked to enter your password.

3. Check the information displayed about the content and permissions of the profile.

4. Tap "Settings" in the upper right corner.

5. If prompted, enter your password.

6. Read the warning message about profile installation and press "Install" again to confirm.

7. After installation, click "Done" to close the installation dialog box.

**Remove a Configuration Profile:**

1. Open the Settings app on your iPhone.

2. Scroll down and tap on "General. "

3. Tap "VPN & Device Management" (or "Profile and Device Management" on older iOS versions).

4. You will see a list of installed profiles. Tap the profile you want to delete.

5. Click "Delete profile".

6. If prompted, enter your password.

7. Confirm the deletion by tapping "Delete" again in the confirmation dialog box.

*By following these steps, you can easily install or remove configuration profiles on your iPhone if needed. Remember that deleting a profile deletes all settings, apps, and data associated with it. Remember to review the profile content before installing or removing it to avoid any unintended changes to your device configuration.*

# SAFETY AND HANDLING

## Important Safety

## Information for iPhone

*WARNING:* Failure to follow these safety instructions could result in fire, electric shock, injury, or damage to iPhone or other property. It is essential to read all safety information provided below before using iPhone.

The safety information provided for iPhone includes several important points to ensure safe and proper use of the device. Here is a summary of key safety instructions:

1. **Handling:** Handle iPhone carefully to avoid damaging its components, especially metal, glass, and plastic. Avoid using iPhone with cracked glass to avoid injury.

2. **Repair:** Only qualified technicians should repair iPhone to avoid damage or injury. The use of non-genuine parts may affect the safety and functionality of the device.

3. **Battery:** iPhone batteries should only be repaired by a qualified technician to avoid overheating, fire, or injury. Dispose of batteries properly according to local environmental laws.

4. **Laser:** Some iPhone models contain a laser beam and improper repair or modification could result in hazardous exposure, causing injury to the eyes or skin.

5. **Distraction:** Using iPhone in certain situations can cause you to lose concentration and lead to dangerous

situations. Comply with rules and
regulations regarding the use of
mobile devices, especially when
driving.

6. **Navigation:** Use caution when using
navigation features as maps and
location-based information may not
always be accurate or available.

7. **Charging:** Follow the correct
charging procedure to avoid fire,
electric shock, or damage to iPhone.
Use only genuine or certified cables
and adapters.

8. **Hearing loss:** Listening to sounds at high volume can cause hearing damage. Set a maximum volume limit and avoid prolonged exposure to high volumes.

9. **Exposure to radio frequencies:** iPhone emits radio signals and while complying with regulations, minimize exposure where possible.

10. **Medical Device Interference:** Magnets and electromagnetic fields from iPhone and accessories may

interfere with medical devices. Please consult medical device manufacturers for advice.

11. **Repetitive Movements:** Using iPhone for long periods of time for repetitive activities may cause discomfort or injury. Please rest and consult your doctor if necessary.

12. **Highly efficient operation:** Do not rely on iPhone in cases where failure could lead to serious consequences.

13.**Choking hazard:** Some iPhone accessories can pose a choking hazard for small children. Keep them out of reach of children.

*By following these safety guidelines, users can minimize risks and ensure safe and proper use of their iPhone devices.*

# Important Handling Information for iPhone

Here is important handling information for iPhone:

1. **Cleaning:** Clean iPhone immediately if it comes into contact with anything that could cause stains or damage, e.g. such as dirt, ink, makeup, soap or acidic substances. Use a soft, slightly damp, lint-free cloth and avoid getting moisture in any gaps. Do not use detergents or compressed air as they may damage the iPhone.

2. **Exposure to liquids and dust:** Wipe away liquid spills or dust with a soft, lint-free cloth. Minimize exposure to liquids, dust and certain substances to avoid damage. Avoid immersing iPhone in water or exposing iPhone to high-velocity water, and stay away from humid environments.

3. **Using connectors, ports and buttons:** Never force connectors into ports or apply excessive force to buttons as this may cause damage not covered by warranty. Make sure the

connectors match the ports and are positioned correctly. Regularly check and clean USB-C or Lightning connectors.

4. **Operating Temperature:** iPhone is designed to operate in ambient temperatures between 32° and 95° F (0° and 35° C) and stored between - 4° to 113° F ( -20° to 45° C). Avoid exposing iPhone to temperature changes or extreme humidity. If iPhone gets too hot, it may stop charging or display a temperature warning screen.

*Following these guidelines will help ensure safe and proper use of your iPhone, minimizing the risk of damage or malfunction.*

*Have fun using your iPhone!*

www.ingramcontent.com/pod-product-compliance
Lightning Source LLC
LaVergne TN
LVHW051346050326
832903LV00030B/2884